Words of One, Volume Six

# Words of One.

Volume Six

By Sophia Love

ISBN – 978-1-7371185-2-7

All books published by Off World Publications ©

www.amazon.com/author/sophialove

Cover art by Tom Wundrak, Fine Art

# Other Works

**The Guardian,** 2016

**Inclusion,** 2017

**sī bôrg,** 2017

**Join me on a Love Quest,** 2018

**The Imposter,** 2019

**Words of One. All Volumes,** 2020/2021


Visit *www.sophialove.org* for these and more.

# Table of Contents

Introduction

Foreword

# Introduction

You hold the transcription of an ongoing conversation with the being I have come to identify as One. It is written here as it was heard telepathically. These conversations have been going on since 2012. They are shared now due to their current focus; this extraordinary year we navigate together. Use your discernment with them, please. Since you've found your way to these pages, there is more than likely some benefit for you in reading them.

Subsequent conversations will be shared in future Volumes.

With blessings and love,
*Sophia*
*2020.5.31*


"There are moments when the collective rises together to a new day, in order to orchestrate and perform a new song. This telling will enliven these moments for you, filling in the blank spots and offering truth. The rising, awakening and Ascension of Man has been foretold. It happens in real time. This time. Your time. Now."

*One*
*2021.8.16*

# Foreword

Since this text is the transcription of a conversation, it is crucial to clarify in what ways the text has been interpreted to convey emphasis and voice. There are several of these cues, and they are as follows:

**Bold face emphasis is used for extra stress on specific words.** These are not my interpretations of what I heard, but highlighted that way as it came through.

*Italics indicate my own voice (that is, Sophia).* Unless otherwise noted, all regular font face body text is the voice of One.

Footnotes and brackets may also be used during the One's dialogue to clarify contextual confusions.

# Chapter 1. May

# Words of One

It is the One.

Volume Six begins with this conversation.

*What is the subject?*

There are methods utilized, as a society is built, that fuel creation and freedom for the civilization. These are advanced tools, known by those of you who incarnate here now.

You have seen these work elsewhere. In other times and at other places and with different beings. We've mentioned before that you are not new to this work. **You came for this work.**

Once the confusion subsides a bit and you are looking at what appears to be the crumbling wreckage of an organized and civil world, you will see that it is, instead, the dust of something pretending to be organized and civil. In actuality, it was a façade, an effective façade.

Looking through it will illustrate what is next, what is needed as correction. It will take a bit for the dust to settle so that you can see clearly.

Use this time for self-care and to see accurately. Oneness will surface. Self-care becomes an inclusive statement of "other".

There will be a lessening of dependence and an increase in focus on giving to **other;** other as an extension of self.

You are not meant to suffer or to proceed alone. Oneness will rise to the surface in this next re-building phase. It will do so out of necessity. It will manifest as truth.

There is no place for evil or slavery to continue in your new world. The conditions, the frequency, the atmosphere itself will not promote it or see it as a viable option.

This takes a while to settle in as truth. There are humans still who only know engagement at such a level. Things have to be cleared out and things have to be **clear.** Once they are, the next steps are seen and they include:

Autonomy
Freedom
Collaboration
Abundance
Prosperity
Joy
Independence
Community
Self-rule
Empowerment
Bliss
Inspiration
Fairness
Compassion
Mutual fulfillment

# Words of One

Your world will mirror what is true rather than what has been portrayed as necessary. It will be messy for a while, as agreements for how to proceed take priority and **this takes time.**

This next segment of the human's journey is a "roll up your sleeves" portion. You are each asked to participate, regardless of age or location. This requires sight. This requires clarity. This requires universal love.

This is a big heal; a moment of restoration.

There are so many wounds. There are so many casualties.

There will be some who say "all is lost". This will be a cue for you to say — "Actually, all is found." You have been lost for generations. The truth has been outed and now you are seeing clearly.

Yes, there have been horrors and abuses.

No, these are not continuing today.

Allow for these horrors to be realized and let them remain in the past. These are truths about what is possible to occur.

The "alien invasion" that's been staged now to fool the population has actually occurred much earlier. It occurred long ago and has been costly.

It is over.

The mental gymnastics it will take to make sense of, and then work successfully with, this information, are not simple. You are well equipped for them *(the mental gymnastics)* however, and ready.

Allow for healing, yet do not stop. Forward movement with intent to unify is necessary now.

It will require a coming together at the heart level first.

It is time to heal. Seeing the source of the anguish is necessary so that healing is focused and complete.

Your next steps are to nourish and allow; to comfort.

Strength, ever-present, will emerge from this wound once it has healed.

Allow for the healing, however uncomfortable this makes you.

Allow.

Allow.

Allow.

That is all.

*Thank you.*

# Words of One

It is the One.

It is an appropriate moment to speak about education. This is a topic you will be considering as you rebuild. The existing system of education is run by monopolies and hierarchies of power. These can be described with a term you have used often – the deep state controllers.

As you conceptualize your society without the restraints and underscored narrative of the old one (*the old society*), you'll be faced with a choice. There are specifics to this choice when discussing different subjects – yet under them all, is a common thread:

"What is the reason for organized education?"

You may want to start by removing the word "organized" and replacing the question with:

"What is the reason for education?"

Here are some thoughts to consider. The initial definition of educate means "to draw out". This is diametrically opposite to mandatory schooling in its current form – which operates entirely "to put in".

We could almost stop there, but there are deeper considerations. This discussion will not be a dissection of just what the current education system is designed "to put in". [1]

Instead, we will focus on the future. The future of education. The care of the next generation of young minds. The purpose, if indeed there is one, to consider instilling a system of organized education in a society at all.

What does it mean: "to draw out"?

The definition assumes there is something there to begin with, (*something within the student*). And that, my dear human, is a great place to start.

Humans are born with an innate knowing. Curiosity is aroused with sensation. Your senses are the doorway to wisdom. There is a necessary entrance point, and this is different for everyone. [2]

There are basic concepts. These are necessary to relate to and operate when in a physical environment.

Answers as to "how many?" and "how big?" and other descriptions of size and content and feeling, only begin to describe the concepts to be aware of here. These are basics. They can easily be taught inside an umbrella of either cooking, or planting, or building, or fixing, or art, for example.

Communication around these is common (*frequently used*) and so language is important to develop.

---

[1] *Clear impression here was "that should be obvious at this point".*
[2] *Here are the possibilities that we are aware of now: sight, hearing, smelling, tasting, touching, feeling. Perhaps in our new world there will be others!*

# Words of One

The body needs care and clothing and maintenance and there are tried and true methods for these that can be shared.

Reading is necessary, as is writing.

With the internet, virtually all pieces of information that are publicly available can be located and perused for accuracy once found.

What is implied by this is an idea. It revolves around simplicity, necessity, and growth/expansion.

What is true when planting seeds for the most abundant growth is that it is necessary to leave plenty of room, nourish generously and utilize the sunlight according to natural cycles/rhythms. You will not yield much if what you are doing is stuffing them into an already crowded area with a minimum of room and nourishment.

Growth, by and large, doesn't need to be tested for. It can be witnessed. It can be demonstrated in the performance of living life.

It is necessary to list the primary component of the current compulsory education program:

Standardized tests to indicate rank.

This amounts to a system of "grading", where the students at the "top" are those whose natural inclination for intellectual data are utilized, (*and thus, they perform well*). It says nothing about the myriad of other "gifts" held by students; things like social, mechanical, artistic, emotional, spiritual, empathic, creative, intuitive, and athletic gifts, to name a few.

This has been a rambling.

What is suggested by its content is that if society continues to decide in favor of mandatory schooling, what exists currently will not be sustainable in its form, as it functions today.

The frequency won't hold it. The children won't cooperate with it. The newly formed systems of society won't require anything that comes from it.

Considerations for programs in self-directed learning will work better for society and for the children. Practical knowledge will need to be passed on, yes. Yet specific direction for success will be more effectively "drawn out", rather than forced in and ranked.

We speak here of a society with love as a base blueprint, rather than control and manipulation. We speak here of your new earth. Its aspects will be your focus in the coming time. Its specific systems will all require an uptick and change.

For although humanity has been changing and will be altered – the governing structures within each society and community will have to be moved into a new method of doing things. This won't naturally, or organically occur.

Change in everything is to be expected and encouraged. You will not successfully function **in any form of regimentation or conformity** that was set up in this 3D matrix.

You are about to hold full control of the wheel.

## Words of One

This becomes your next task. Your destination will be determined by the map you are following. Now it is upon you to draw that map.

That is all.

*Thank you.*

**May 20, 2021**
6:40 AM

It is the One, Sophia.

*Thank you.*

Our discussion now revolves around what it is you can do to eliminate fear. For it is insidious, constant and everywhere.

It is hiding within "anger".

It is a part of "safety".

It comes out in "righteousness".

It demonstrates itself most clearly in shows of aggression and power over.

Fear has become a sort of go to emotion on earth. It is what runs the society.

There are situations where fear is appropriate. It instills action. These situations that necessitate fear can be compared to being chased by something that means to harm you. Fear increases adrenaline, which accelerates your speed; very necessary and helpful.

Yet fear has crept into daily life. It can exist as a relentless force, raising anxiety to a continuous and ever-present level.

# Words of One

Fear is not helpful when it exists as a constant. Anxiety is a driving force beneath illness, as well as self-destructive habits.

In order to replace fear with love, it will need to be seen. It will need to be recognized once it is seen. It will need to be understood.

Daily life is a series of choices…

> Will you get out of bed or stay?
> Will you exercise or linger over a cup of coffee?
> What clothing will you put on?
> What activity will you start your day with?
> What will you eat?

These are presented always as physical life's options. They become, or the answers to them become, habits or surprises and vehicles for change.

They sound small and inconsequential, yet we've named only a few in order to illustrate the constant presence of choice.

Choice motivates action. The emotion beneath choice comes into play here, and affects not only the decision, but the chemical and physiological make-up of your body.

If you jump out of bed because you have "over-slept" and are now afraid you'll be late for work, your body is running on a chemical cocktail that speeds everything up. If you then grab a cup of coffee in order to remain alert, and perhaps a sweet roll – you've added sugar and caffeine to that cocktail.

Each decision you make after that initial one, which was fear inspired (you jumped out of bed) will be colored by the effects of that chemical cocktail.

Fear can and does become addictive. It can be used as a sort of go-to emotion in order to feel as if you are doing something, something productive or correct or powerful.

**Fear is never conquered. It is placated**, ready to arise when necessary (think of that being chased by a large animal scenario).

It is not necessary as a driving and constant emotion.

It will be available if that large animal shows up. That is a guarantee.

You have been raised in a world that is filled with imaginary large animals. They look like potentials...

Possible illness.
Possible failure.
Possible poverty.
Possible pain.
Possible loss.

What you have never been told, truthfully told, is of your own power. This has been an intentional omission. Once you recognize that the fear that fills your emotional reservoir is brought on by imaginary large animals, you can begin to get a hold of it.

This is not to say that bad things aren't real or even possible. This is to say that to move always in ways that will avert a potential and dangerous threat is a damaging effort, not a nourishing one. This wears on your psyche and your body without you realizing it. This ages you pre-maturely. This sets the stage for illness.

If instead, you focus on the word "imaginary" and refute the warnings that society have been shouting, you will begin to feel some control.

For your imagination is your most powerful tool and the key to creation. We have spoken of this before.

It is the reason for all the fear-mongering, fear-porn, fear-scenarios. These are laid out before you as entertainment, medical announcements, warnings. They assume a place in your mind, and can instill fearful images.

What you can do, is to take control of your mind's images. Take control of what has taken residence there, "rent free" as it were. Evict those that are reducing the property value, and invite/create new occupants that promote things desired. Things like health, happiness, prosperity, strength, community, world peace, abundance, advancement, love, joy, inspiration.

These are every bit as vital as what you've been told, more so actually. Your focus has been intentionally directed to keep you afraid and obedient to the loudest and scariest potentials of life.

Instead, and now, you will be better served by changing it to look at other things. Things that are also possible and potential outcomes. You'll have to hold your gaze on these things.

As your existing structures crumble, it is your collective imagination that forms the blueprint for new structures. You are an individual part of that collective. Dreams, visions, thoughts and ideas of freedom, prosperity, peace and vitality are building blocks.

Hold these close and constant. Replace the old narratives with potentials that please you. This is how a new world is built. Not by refusing to look at fear, but by placing it in its appropriate spot, to be pulled out when that large animal shows up.

Love is what builds the next world, your new earth and the life you dream of.

You will find your power there. You will see, dear human, you will see.

That is all.


*Thank you.*

# Words of One

**May 21, 2021**
2:47 AM

It is the One.

Some things are happening right now that indicate who is running things for the most part. You do not see these, yet there are planned announcements for them.

These approach.

They will be a surprise for everyone whether or not you are paying attention.

For those of you in anticipation for "something", these are the moments that you will always recall in which "something" did indeed occur. You'll remember both the anticipation and the moment in which it stopped.

It is this way for sensitives and not-so-sensitives alike. The tension is palpable.

Here it is time to give you an idea of what it is you sense. A change so massive that it is felt by everyone and will affect everyone. This is a change in the order of things, in the matrix as perceived by you, in the very fabric of your reality.

This is a correction.

It cannot be done subtly.

It cannot be hidden from human eyes.

It is an alteration.

You could even call it a "changing of the guard". Although, what approaches and it is changing into, is not a new guard so much as a new frequency and some who are more compatible with this frequency.

It is the frequency of love. It is not the frequency of fear and control.

As it (the change in frequency) is felt in full force, there will be a palpable shift. It will be experienced physically.

You cannot envision this as you've never lived within a base vibration that was not fear based.

I tell you this.

You will rejoice here once you adjust. The sense of freedom will be palpable and visceral.

Freedom is love's true expression.

Joy is love's base emotion.

These are things you had to create in your recent life, in your history, indeed in mankind's history.

These things will be where you begin, the core of every imagining and the ink with which you pen your blueprint for the creation of

# Words of One

your life.

This control matrix will switch off.

This is your sense and the thing that you all anticipate.

It feels threatening, yet I tell you it will not be painful.

Ultimately, it is the foundation for bliss.

When it happens, and there will be no doubt about it when it does, remain in happiness and feel the sense of control that accompanies it. For those of you who look always for outside authority, it will be a bit of a jolt.

It need not be.

Awareness should help to alleviate that, and allow more of "going with the flow".

It will be a joyous ride then.

That is all.

You are in for such a treat, my dear, dear human.


*Thank you.*

**May 22, 2021**
4:24 AM

It is the One.


*Is there anything to say today?*


There are several topics that could be discussed. A decision about them is being made now.

Today we will discuss money and its presence or absence in your life. Not absence in the way typically thought of, as in poverty. But absence in the idea of a society that doesn't utilize it at all. This concept is a foreign one to you, for money is all that you have ever known.

If you go back in recorded history, you will see that there has always been present some sort of accumulation of wealth. There have always been counting houses. There have been banks. There have been money lenders. These ideas seem normal to you, as do the vast quantities of gold and jewels that are held in depictions of ancient temples and places of royalty. It is considered mere fact, not something that needs to be questioned.

Let us speak of the concept of money. It is utilized by you as a means of exchange. Yet, recently, it is losing its monetary value and its power to purchase/exchange has become compromised. It does not hold in value.

This idea of value is something you've been taught. Money has been introduced into the society, into your world, as a tool. A tool always meant to divide you, separate you by a specific distinction; those who have a large amount of value and those who are wanting.

It is a trap of dependence, of which there is no escape. Money is one of the primary gears running the course of life for you here.

In contrast, let us look at what society could look like without it. For you, this will be an imaginary idea. Yet there are many, many worlds without money. One day, earth will be one of them.

Without money there are no concepts of prosperity, wealth, poverty or enslavement. They are structured in such a way that allows life to be a natural progression of personal development, community and worldly involvement, and collective advancement, progress and joy.

Imagine being born into a place that held no concept of invented division by wealth accumulation. Imagine being born and having all of your needs met in such a way that was sufficient for health and growth and happiness and fulfillment. Where you expected to always have food, water, clothing, housing, comfort and happiness, because **everywhere you looked this was the case.**

Imagine growing up without the pressure of needing to train for a "good paying" "job". Where you could successfully follow your passions and support yourself.

Imagine never worrying about the status of your bank account or your retirement.

Imagine not needing more money to purchase better food, clothing, housing or medical treatment.

Such a society would hold no concepts of rich or poor as indicated by how many bits of paper or gold your bank account held. Such a society would have a completely other concept of value.

In it, value would not be monetized, or dependent on something "needed" from someone or something who "has it". Value would not be dependent on some outside other to grant it to you.

Value would have to come from something else.

And what else is there?

There is you.

Value would come from you.

If there were no labels of rich or poor, all of the society's members would be looked at as equally worthy. Worthy of the same access to whatever is available.

In such a world there would be incentives to work for the sake of betterment for the whole. Advancements in any arena would benefit the whole, not just the rich who could "afford it".

Without an idea of money, you would have access to whatever you needed, whenever you needed it. There would be no concept of "want", because of this. No-one would be left without. There is an implied equality of value in such a plan – you are each equally worthy.

# Words of One

There are so many differences between a world set up this way and your current earthly model. Yet I will leave you with just one. For know that the earth one day will run in entirely new ways and money is a large part of that change.

**Consider a world where the mere fact that you are born and alive is enough.**

Where you expect abundance and fulfillment and home and health, in the same way you today expect oxygen. It is everywhere, and always yours.

The concept of freedom in such a world revolves around equality of value. Life has value and that value is not able to be ranked higher or lower on some sort of chart. That value exists the moment you are born and is a constant.

This is the society you will build in your new world.

It is the eventual goal. Today's monetary crashes and changes in form are the pre-cursors for that.

Know that as money changes from paper to quantum, so do ideas about accumulation, worth and value. It will be some time before "no money at all" is how society is structured, yet it is an inevitable outcome.

Ideas around self-worth need to be expanded and awakened before you get there. This requires healing and, in some cases, re-education.

It is the current members of the race that need the healing and, in some cases, re-education regarding worth and value. The newest ones do not. They are born knowing their value and will demonstrate an ease with accepting yours as well.

This is how your society will evolve.

It is a gradual, beautiful process and one you will witness.

Look forward to these next steps, dear human. You are bound to enjoy them immensely.

*That is all.*

# Words of One

**May 23, 2021**
3:00 AM

It is the One.

There are things to say.

*I have a few questions.*

Go ahead Sophia.

*There are continuing questions about the MRNA vaccines and their effect; their effect on 50+ year old people. Also, facts about the shedding effect on un-vaccinated people in close contact. These are specific medical questions.*

Specific medical reactions will depend on the health, physiology and intent of the life path of the person in question. These vaccines are not what they purport to be, most certainly. There is another agenda with their wide distribution. Yet individual responses will vary and these occur at every age.

The vaccine is equally problematic at every age. Individual immune system responses will vary. It can be said that the very young and the very old are the most vulnerable. Everyone in between these two extremes will differ. By "very young" is meant not yet birthed.

The preponderance of light in children protects them.

*Thank you.*

*Would you comment on Israel and the newly resurrected conflict there?*

Political posturing always changes the landscape and this is much of what is seen now. Any leader who promotes the sacrifice of his own for these aspirations is not working for the light. In order to discern who is who right now, it will assist to look at the effect of their actions. Who is harmed? Who is protected?

There are favors being called in. Also, there is deep compromise.

These things provoke the waking up of the populace and in some cases that is the end goal. There are deals being made and images/public images being either preserved or crafted.

This is a play, a show. The land hosting this current conflict is always in play for control. There are sacred and powerful sites there. Countries who control them then command their power.

Let it be said that at this late date this pretense of ownership and conflict over who holds what is inconsequential.

The light has taken hold. You witness the fallout. When the dust settles, it will all be clear.

Things have not changed so much as they are being staged.

# Words of One

*Okay.*

*Thank you.*

**May 24, 2021**
4:00 AM

It is the One.

Things to say now have to do with your liberation.

Things to say now have to do with the process itself.

For the bulk of the race does not consider itself enslaved, not in the way that it is. And that is the issue. There will be a massive amount of truth unleashed, followed by a great unlearning.

For the race has learned well, and this is part of the attraction. [3] Humanity is a quick study and highly adaptable.

What will be the most difficult to unlearn and then adapt to, will be the identities of people that you either trusted or mis-trusted. It will be a challenge to trust anyone at all for a while; any public figure that is. There will be many surprises.

What is about to occur, and is a necessary part of the process, is a re-examination of what you believed, who you believed, and why. This will eventually move inward, to self, and become an examination of self.

For this is evolution. Your Ascension and awakening occur on a macro-cultural-planetary level and on a micro-individual level. You are changing, re-forming and renewing everything. Nothing will be untouched or un-examined on the journey.

---

[3] *Meaning the attraction to humans on earth; why other beings are so drawn to the race.*

# Words of One

This idea of trust is bound to trigger internal chaos. Realize, when confusion and despair is felt, that you've been living in a control matrix. In it, you had everything around you set up and structured to point you in certain and specific directions.

These directions were followed, not because of any inherent weakness or fault on your part. The illusion was a convincing one. It was expertly crafted by a race who has done this for thousands of years.

Based on what you saw, heard, felt and lived – you made the decisions you made.

Now, the frequency is different, you are changed as well, and the matrix crumbles.

Now, you are seeing things differently and you are being told additional information with which to decide.

Who to trust?

Who to distrust?

I tell you that your ability to accurately "read" another being will kick-in and be honed to an art. Parts of your DNA were stifled and thus inactive before now. Your intuitive and logical abilities will be, and are now, developing further and becoming enhanced.

All this is to say – you can and you will come **to trust yourself,** and this is where it begins. **You will know truth** when it is in front of you, and you will see through falsehoods. This happens regardless of the "show" around whatever or whoever is dispensing the information.

Trust will change from something you are instructed to do, (because of the position or title that the person instructing you holds), to something you know internally.

Trust is an inner knowing. As it comes to the surface and is accepted as reason for action – a peace grows for you; an inner peace.

What will be initially painful for many will be the confusion around identifying truth.

This now moves from an external stimulus to an internal realization. There are parts of this process that don't appear to make sense, not based on the "rules" you've always followed. They will "go against the grain", and this will feel uncomfortable.

For a while.

Eventually, (and this is an inevitable transition), things will feel more comfortable and authentic than you've ever experienced them. You'll have a truth radar that will be fully activated, and your decisions about what you are hearing, seeing and doing will resonate completely.

Not at first, my dear, dear human, not at first. [4]

---

[4] *What came through here, and throughout the conversation, was that we will feel an internal chaos. This will be centered around the idea of trust. This*

# Words of One

The discomfort you feel upon learning hidden truths, secrets, identities and methods of suppression, is bound to feel overwhelming.

Remember, when this happens, that it is a temporary adjustment and does not last long. You are in the midst of an awakening.

The trajectory leads to full awareness and congruence of emotion and action. Inner conflict eventually becomes non-existent, as you act based on what you, yourself **know** to be in harmony with your belief system. [5]

Full awareness becomes your most comfortable state to be in – eventually. You are learning to trust yourself, my dear human. **This was always about you.**

That is all.

*Thank you.*

Goodbye Sophia, my chosen one.

---

*manifests externally, as chaos in society. It is a simultaneous process and plays out that way. This cannot be helped. As we react and then adjust, so does our world.*
[5] *In harmony with your essence.*

**May 27th, 2021**
5:40 AM

It is the One.

Things have occurred on your planet that are worth discussing. These things concern your military. Very quickly now they will be front and center for you, as the forces in charge actually step into the public view. They've been running things beneath the show.

Unbeknownst to the population, there are many deals, many players, and an orchestrated plan. The purpose of the plan is two-fold.

> First, to draw out every hidden agenda and deep state player; to expose their game and identify them.

> Second, to provide those willing players with opportunities to either save-face or save family members or reduce their own punishment. By having them assist in the take-down and exposure of the dark controllers.

Some of what occurs now will create confusion and even chaos. People will be distraught at the names and actions of their well-known and loved celebrities and political and/or public figures.

Yet this upset/reaction will be an initial one, and relatively brief. It gives away quickly to the absolute horror at the harvesting and control that has been happening here.

The true nature of the agenda here will be exposed soon.

# Words of One

This will shock the world. It will come out in a surprising way, and quickly, once it begins. And (*it will come out*) in a way that cannot be refuted or denied.

It will expose people and programs. Numbers of both are staggering.

Nothing can prepare you for this. It has gone on beneath the actual surface of your planet for a very long time. This is a family business, and the families who run it, who own it, are not names you know.

The history is long and the numbers of humans involved here, on some level, are much larger than you have imagined.

What happens now is a public reversal and eventually, a rectifying of historical abuses and horrors. **The extent to which the race has been used and abused will be matched with this next effort – the reach of healing, prosperity, love, power and joy.**

There is to be a correction.

This could not have happened without evicting the dark ones. They are gone.

Their programs still exist however, and now comes the exposure and public explanation of what happened here.

Humans are in charge of this part. You refer to them in many ways – white hats, the Alliance, etc. This is a world-wide effort.

This is a decades long plan.

It has been helped by off-world players.

It has been helped with quantum technology.

What will be made public will be the path taken of the players, and their motive.

Money will be at the core of it. Money and control.

The real evil here, as adopted and perpetrated by humans, begins with separation. Value and worth have been assigned according to genetics. This inherent falsehood has propelled every hierarchy and nation-state.

The secret beneath what you've learned about your history is that there is a "hidden hand" writing everything you've learned. None of it is based on discovered truth. All of it is a story – told to manipulate. Told to control. In some cases, planting seeds that would not germinate for generations, for hundreds of years.

What you are to see played out publicly is a bit of a mess, and will appear confusing.

**Someone will play the final card to get the ball rolling. It must be played.**

Those in control now are poised and prepared for this moment.

They have seen it with their technology. It will be shocking.

This has been delayed and adjusted so many times, yet is inevitable.

# Words of One

Know that all is well, whatever you see happening in Washington or on Wall Street. This will not end badly and is not the end.

It is the beginning.

The military step forward. There is what appears to be a military take-over. This is global.

These words are to prepare you. Know that it has to play out this way in order to seize back control of every element lost to the deep state. Once it happens, it happens quickly.

Centuries of ownership are being reversed here. The few months it takes for the dust to settle are but a brief moment by comparison.

The public will be told the story of who has done what, and why.

Not all details of the horror will be broadcast on your nightly news initially. But they will come out and be told eventually.

There must be a re-learning.

There has to be acceptance.

There will be a coming together of humanity. This will not be stopped.

When the military take center stage, you are seeing the last act.

Do not fall into fear.

There are bound to be casualties and surprises. Remember that free will trumps all, and runs the show. At any point, and up until the very last second, a mind can be changed and another choice made. For everyone. By everyone.

The inevitability of the joyous ending for humanity carries this show forward to its natural conclusion. There are numerous paths, yet one destination.

The military is not your enemy.

The former controllers are being escorted off stage and, in some cases, off planet. It takes a unified and world-wide effort to accomplish this.

Patience on your part will be required for a while still. Not for years, but for months.

You will see the conclusion in your lifetime.

You will see an end to the tyrannical control within a year.

The effort to rebuild begins already, and comes into full view once the military leaves center stage.

This will never re-occur on earth. Your new world begins with the death of the old. It is the only way.

You'll need to nurture all seeds and potentials for growth. There will be a great healing. Your *(new)* leaders are stepping forward already for this.

# Words of One

Remain clear of fear and full of gratitude for what has been and is being accomplished.

You've done it, my dear, dear human.

You've anchored the light. Its hold here is solid. You've prepared a place for the birth of your new world. This is a joyous moment indeed.

Rejoice and know that it is done.

That is all.


*Thank you.*


Goodbye Sophia, my scribe.

**May 31, 2021**
4:26 AM

It is the One.


*Thank you.*


What we have to talk about now are topics that concern who you are and why you are here.

"You" personally.

"You" empirically.

For there are multitudes of reasons for life. And there are multitudes of descriptions for the effect that life has on the time in which it is taken.

You exist as a physical being, living in a specific time; a projection of form living on a specific place.

You exist just as you have envisioned yourself to exist. You are carrying out your individual plan for life within a collective construct of reality. What never changes inside of that plan is your unique spark; your individual purpose for appearing at all.

Circumstances around you change, as timelines adjust and respond to collective responses.

# Words of One

**You do not.**

**Your original purpose does not.**

You appeared as human in this now moment on earth for very specific and individual reasons. Each of these has to do with your evolution.

You came to experience a facet of physical life that you felt you needed. The reasons you felt you needed to be here are as unique as you are. In some cases, they are similar to each other. In all cases they will benefit your overall development.

Those of you who've found your way to these words have been here before. By "here" is meant to a physical existence while being aware of your non-physical nature.

This is not your first rodeo.

What is different this "time" is that many of you share a common purpose. It is not your only purpose. It is one of them.

This is the purpose that asks you to wake up the collective to the illusion in which they are. This is the purpose of a collective Ascension – an evolutionary springboard to full awareness while physical.

It is a precious moment, unique in its own way due to the human being's long exposure to the earth's enslavement regime.

The fact of the regime change is an unalterable one. The participation you enjoy within that change is one you have intended.

In other words – this freeing of the race occurs. It occurs now. Its occurrence is not optional or possible to change. Your participation in its occurrence is and has been part of the plan always.

In this way, you are a necessary cog in the wheel. A part needed for its success. A part contributing to its success, regardless of what circumstances look like around you.

You are necessary.

You are at full choice.

Creation is similar to a machine, or a living organism. It moves forward, carries on, operates and functions the most optimal way it can with whatever components it has that are currently functioning.

It works as a single unit – accommodating for each part as it does.

There are no unnecessary components in creation.

There are no useless moments or insignificant parts.

All of creation contributes to the whole.

It is in this way it can be said that all of creation contributes to the light.

Contrast is necessary to appreciate full brilliance.

Darkness exposes possibilities.

# Words of One

All action exists as a sort of mechanism to keep the parts moving.

There is never a goal to eliminate a portion of creation. In truth, this cannot be accomplished.

The goal is always and consistently to support the whole.

Darkness exists.

It exists as a component of contrast.

Conflict occurs when an imbalance skews things. When that occurs, life "suffers" and appears to be eliminated at a greater proportion than it is being promoted.

You are here now, on earth, witnessing and participating in this physical evolutionary liberation for personal and global reasons. You are here to aid the process of Ascension. You may also be here to investigate...

Forgiveness
Gratitude
Love
Anger
Pain
Prosperity
Poverty
Illness
Generosity
Greed
Cruelty

Compassion
Wealth
Need
Fortitude
Patience
Independence
Responsibility
Humbleness
Arrogance
Dependence
Laziness
Aggression
Weakness
Selfishness
Devotion
Simplicity

There is a myriad of experiences available. These play out with acquaintances, family members, friends and lovers.

It always comes to personal interaction. These can be random "one-off" moments that occur while making your way to what you think is the point of it all – a job or event that predominates your life at the moment. You may not even notice one of these seemingly small interactions with another.

Yet I tell you – nothing is insignificant. Any conflict that inspires thought, action or response carries consequences that then effect the course you follow.

There are no random actions. The entire body of creation conspires and adjusts so that you fulfill your purpose for being part of it at all.

It is a continuous moving machine/organism to which you hold the wheel. The wheel to your life – it is all relevant. For your life – every moment advances you one step closer to the point of your participation.

The personal point.

The collective point.

There are no inconsequential moments. [6] You are at choice to ignore them as they present themselves to you – or – to fully engage in them, appreciating their offering.

As the frequency increases, you will, no doubt, notice and participate consciously with each interaction as you notice it.

Consciousness means increased awareness. The faster frequency presents you with more options to which you can become aware. These will present as previously unseen participants come into view. You will be seeing more.

These are not "ghosts", but other life forms. They've been here always.

As your frequency increases, you become aware of more, of "others" who exist at your new frequency. You do not lose those

---

[6] *Note – just at this moment a flock of geese flew overhead, very close and very loud! Encouraging each other with each honk. Sophia*

who seem to be stuck at a different rate – you just move differently than they do. Aware of each other still, means that there is a purpose to the contact.

Do not make the mistake of believing that it is always the one who is most conscious who is here to teach. For you may be missing out on something vital to your evolution.

Pay attention.

Pay attention to it all.

For, like that flock of geese, you are here on a collective journey, shouting encouragement to each other, aiding the ones who seem to be having the most difficult position with the toughest go of it. You are all doing the same thing.

You are here to propel your evolution; your collective evolution and your personal growth.

One does not happen in isolation. There is a seamless and gorgeous synchronicity to creation. This can be witnessed once you step back far enough.

It is easy to miss if you are in the midst of it – close and intensely participating. Yet, it is present always. A synchronized, self-regulating movement propelling the whole to its intended destination.

There are no delays or mistakes in creation. There are adjustments and new approaches always as a response to the whole. Each component necessary. Every part chosen.

# Words of One

It will help you to realize in the coming days that all of your interactions are significant. They are potential learning experiences, whether noticed or ignored. If ignored, they will undoubtedly be presented again. The option to learn from them is always yours – free will is a constant. [7]

Having come with a specific goal, the mechanism of your life will present and present and present again the lesson sought. This continues until it is received or you exit the program.

Age does not alter the purpose chosen.

The collective envisioning does not alter the purpose chosen.

In this way, you can appreciate those repetitive thoughts and/or relationships, and/or circumstances of your life as necessary and meaningful. If you are in resistance, it will feel uncomfortable.

What will help is ease and allowing. Notice, and with an open heart, welcome each interaction. It occurs for you, is noticed by you, and can now be utilized to enhance and fulfill your life's goals.

Your life is enriched with interaction, with more life. It is intended that you move **toward** each other for fulfillment – **not away.** You are here together for a reason. If you did not require the interaction, you would not be having it.

Notice everything.

_____

[7] *Note – again the geese flew overhead but this time they were further away...*

It all matters.

Take from it, what you can digest, and then notice the next.

Your life is enriched in this way, with each small, seemingly insignificant moment.

Fulfillment cannot be plotted or arranged with ego.

Fulfillment occurs through connection.

Life itself then answers every question. Remain conscious always of the inquiry. In this way, you will not suffer boredom or pointlessness in your days.

Keep moving always.

That is all.


*Thank you.*


Goodbye Sophia, my chosen one. [8]

---

[8] *Note — A flock of geese flew overhead one last time as One closed this conversation. Three of them in total this morning.*

# Words of One

# Chapter 2. June

# Words of One

**June 2, 2021**
5:20 AM

It is the One.

These are times of great duress. These are painful times, times in which the global mood cries out for a quick ending and return to some sort of normal. To some place that is not filled with worry about what may be around the next corner, the next day, or instigated by the next person.

I tell you this.

These emotions are experienced now as a way of empathizing with your fellow humans who have spent much of their lives, perhaps all of their lives, captured. You are becoming a global voice. While largely still unaware of specific details – you carry and express identical emotion at a pretty much constant rate. These include…

Fear
Uncertainty
Apprehension
Discomfort
Distrust
Anxiety
Exhaustion

As you process these, in varying degrees and daily, you unify. You unify in comprehension. You unify in appreciation.

For these are the constant companions of slaves. Slavery is a global condition.

Although you have not been "stolen", and you walk around "free", your climate, your movements, your possibilities for expression are controlled and limited. They are now limited in an obvious "in your face" way with lockdowns, mandates, regulations and masks.

It is important to realize that although the control is only obvious now – **it has been here always.** This is a brilliantly enacted plan that utilized an illusion to convince you otherwise. **The creation of an alternate narrative will have to be as constant and as convincing as the initial one.**

In this effort, you are aided by both the current frequency (the old ways cannot be sustained any longer) and the current climate (exhaustion, frustration, fear). People are getting done with this. People are ready for change.

You are almost there. Until and unless the global voice says, out loud, "no more" – there will exist pockets of acceptance as an antidote to change. This ("no more") has to be the majority. A unified "no" must be stated.

It is one thing to feel defeated because of conditions in your life. It is quite another to feel, instead, determined to change those conditions in whatever way you can.

It is the latter that predominates the collective right now.

What differs is the "how". Those who are still believing the given narrative as true, will be complying with all proposed health mandates, and gladly doing so for relief and a sense of normal.

61

# Words of One

Those who, on the other hand, do not believe the given narrative as true, are opposing the health mandates while demanding the same relief and return to normal movement.

Similar emotions. Different responses to them.

You will have to come together in order to emanate a global proclamation for action.

You've come together in emotion. You've maintained a split with your actions.

What actually occurs now, and it is a step towards unity, is comprehension for the reasons of each other's actions.

This is due to love.

You love each other more than you disagree.

This beautiful process of your unification is happening organically and naturally, due to the common condition of the virus. It is the stimulus that invited unification.

What comes next is another stimulus.

This is mentioned here as a way of warning and announcement. There are two contributing factors to the stimulus for further unity. Both originate beyond the human family.

One begins with the owners/the controllers themselves. They are not fully human. In some cases, they are not human at all.

The second is divine intervention.

There will be no predictions in "time" for these events. There will only be this… A general statement as a way of warning. When either event occurs, this statement made now will inform you as to what it is you are looking at.

Regardless of how convincing the stimulus is from the dark ones — it is not successful in their stated purpose and falling into fear is not helpful. Remember that this heralds **their** ending and not humanity's (ending).

Remember, there is a divine moment that captures the attention of humanity and tells you truth.

Both herald the end.

Both announce the beginning.

Regardless of what things look like, know that they are temporary, and know that you came here, to this lifetime, on earth in 2021, with full awareness.

You are ready.

The worst is over. You have deemed it so.

The best is on its way.

There are some among you who came as very specific participants in the coming days. Warriors, who have waited until now to step

# Words of One

forward. Theirs is a unique and specific ability. Their work is powerful and necessary for these final moments.

You will know them by their signature.

You will recognize their light.

Soon, it will light every corner holding darkness.

Soon, it will be all that you see.

Trust your intuition and know that all is well.

You will come through this effort as ONE. This was always the plan.

It is a unique pleasure to witness humanity craft for itself a method to do this. [9]

Specifically in each life, and globally, as one race, you are expanding your appreciation and empathy for each other. This fortifies and unifies you. Eventually you will feel and see the strength provided in Oneness.

You are in for such a treat, my dear, dear human. What comes next is miraculous.

That is all.

--------

[9] *There was deep appreciation and joy felt here! A smiling face and a twinkle in the eye sort of feeling! Profound love and a sense of pride.*

*Thank you.*

Goodbye my chosen one.

# Words of One

It is the One.

These times need not bring on stress to your instrument. Taking a different approach to bodily care and support will help you to avoid additional pressure and/or negative effect.

Your body has functioned within the same frequency for pretty much its entire existence.

Until now.

This process is asking your physical self to operate in a whole new atmosphere. This affects everything you are attempting to do, each and every day.

Sleeping, eating, walking, working, resting, exercising, playing. All of these things, the activities of life, are continuing as if nothing has changed.

Yet so much is different.

In a new frequency, your body is "sped up" as it moves each day. It cannot help but respond. It cannot help but move in concert with the vibration in which it is swimming.

You will notice some of the following. Perhaps you already have…

Different sleep patterns

Different responses to weather

A faster tempo, even though you do not "see" things moving at a different rate than they once did, you "feel" that they are

Desires for less food, for different food

Thirst

A feeling of spaciousness, even in a crowded room

New sensitivities. These may be to foods, noises, fabrics – even people

Low tolerance for emotional pressure

Rapid adjustment to new programs of thought and/or alternate scheduling

A sense that you are hearing sounds you didn't used to hear, and seeing, more often, things out of the corner of your eye

As the frequency increases, you can't help but respond. It will ease your anxiety to accept whatever shows up as a part of this acceleration, and quite natural.

Avoid frustration by realizing that it is natural and expected. "Go with the flow".

This will mean different things for each of you, as you have had different starting points.

# Words of One

In a general sense, it will serve you to…

Sleep when you are tired

Move with the sunlight, in the sunlight

Feed your body what it craves

*Note – I had to stop here unexpectedly. Sophia*

**June 9, 2021**
5:24 AM

It is the One.

Things are occurring right now on this planet that effect the course of the (human) race. These are hidden from the public view at this point. They will not always be.

It is helpful for you to hear of these things. As you do, and you process their meaning, you'll have a more expanded view.

Part of the process of your expansion is this view. You will incorporate a broader perspective into your seeing, and will have a deeper comprehension of how your life fits. How your life fits into the greater scheme of things. For you are here with purpose. That purpose is both personal and what you might call global.

Once you comprehend your true nature, you'll experience a sense of purpose unlike any you've held thus far. It will feel more complete. It will be more comprehensive.

For your life as a star seed, light worker or truth teller holds an initiatory force for this planetary shift. It is because of you that this happens at all, and because of your presence that it occurs right now.

It's been attempted twice before.

This time, it will be completed.

# Words of One

You came with different skill sets and purposes. On some level, your participation has been part of your life always.

You also came to play out human dramas and lessons, simultaneously pushing forward an agenda. An agenda of evolution. A program of enlightenment. A process that will assist in the Ascension of the (human) race.

What can be said now is this. The cumulative effect of your efforts, the efforts of the star seeds, light workers, truth tellers and light warriors, has yielded an unstoppable wave of destruction, cleansing, and ultimately – nourishment. It is a tidal wave of change. It is pure power.

What this looks like from an earth-bound perspective will be a breaking up of all that has held the matrix society together. The destruction has begun, and it proceeds in earnest. Its cumulative effect will feel massive and shocking. These will be short-lived emotions for those of you here for this. They'll quickly change into calls for action.

You will each instinctively know which action to take.

Do not fall into fear. There are many more of you here for this next part than are currently aware. They will soon be activated. Events, about to transpire, will see to it.

There has been a change in command. A transfer, in this physical realm, of the machinations of control. It is done. It must be played out now in an orderly fashion for humanity to witness.

There will be pushback. Expect unrest and a bit of discomfort, but this will not be long-lived.

You are to see the unfolding of the complete story; the truth. The next ninety days will be like none before them for the compressed effect of massive global alteration.

The narrative changes.

The narrative around health, government, money and control begins its transformation. This happens already behind closed doors.

Yet, prepare for those doors to be blown wide open. You will not end the year in the same fog in which you started it.

The confirmation of command and control has occurred in your military. You will hear of this in whispers and unconfirmed reports. When you do, know that they refer to a true transfer of control.

What needs to be said is this. There are many who are here now to assist. They have been caught up in their life and are not fully conscious of their purpose for this time. The majority of them will be sparked now, will be "turned on" and directed towards their planned role. They will take their place and assist.

The transfer will be messy, yet complete and rapid. This is a global effort.

Know that every inside nudge now will point you closer to where you've intended. It may not appear so outwardly. Trust.

What you will quickly discover is that all systems are go, and the place they are going is one of freedom and peace, prosperity and joy. This is a place ruled by a state of love, not fear. This is the place you are here to usher in, to welcome and to enjoy. This is your new Earth.

It cannot show up in any way but truthfully. Know that when you see or sense falsehoods and deception, you are witnessing the last gasps of what it is you are leaving behind.

Your new Earth will arrive in full transparency – pure and whole. Anything other than that, will not survive, will not continue.

No more lies.

No more deceit.

No more power-over.

You are about to begin an era of power-with and power-full. A combined effort with a single purpose. Oneness.

As you witness the breakdowns and reversals in these coming times, hold on to the fact that all falsehoods must fall before the truth can be revealed.

You will know truth by its frequency. It will take some getting used to, you haven't lived there much.

You are about to.

You will see, dear human, many changes in the coming days. Know that they all lead to a place you've come to build together, as One.

This is a wonderous place and it will be worth every step taken.

You will not be disappointed.

That is all.


*Thank you.*

# Words of One

It is the One.

These are the times of the Great Divide. To be clear, there has been an unrealized divide in the race for centuries. Unrealized by the pure of heart and gentle of soul, but fully realized by those who were not.

With consciousness, this becomes realized. Motivations for action rise to the surface and are exposed. Intentions and purposes are seen clearly.

There is an overall agenda to a life as lived, that overshadows the specifics. This has been labeled "service to self", yet it is even more than that.

For "service to self" may be another way to describe selfishness. What this is, is a life governed by motivation for singular pleasure at the expense of other. This is beyond selfishness or even greed. This is the definition of a socio-path in your psychological literature.

When you read the description, note that they (*meaning sociopaths*) can be charming. Think about the various well known and loved personalities in royalty, government, sport and theater. A charming personality is part of the deception, a costume, an empty covering meant for a role and nothing more.

What will be difficult for many to accept is the truth about their favorite personalities. It will be shocking. It will feel like a deep betrayal and will cause anger as well as grief. Folks will wonder who it is that they can trust and what it is that they can believe?

Here is where true transformation begins.

The race will turn inward to trust themselves. The race will form internally based opinions. And, decisions will come more from how they feel, versus what they've been told.

It will not be an easy transition, as much of your history is upended and reversed. The "bad guys" in many cases, were not who they were painted to be. The "good guys" were, more often than not, stopped and labeled so that the agenda of the controllers could be completed.

These turnarounds of truth will be most upsetting for those well-meaning and pure of heart souls who promoted the narrative in academia. Meaning and much examining has been conducted from outright fabrication.

You have not been told the truth.

You have been kept literally in the dark.

All by some beautiful "important" and well-spoken sociopaths. This is a difficult pill to swallow.

Once digested, you will see the world differently. You will end up having more hope, not less. You will begin to trust your neighbor to a degree that is warranted, by who he is versus what you've been told.

# Words of One

Conditions of poverty and crime will become a status of oppression and virtually disappear in a world of global abundance and equality of opportunity. There are many changes you'll have to make, my dear human, yet the speed and ease with which you do will astound you.

No longer will you be blocked by the controller's agenda of "self at all costs". You will collaborate and mutually benefit.

Systems evolve gradually and in steps, yet in this time you enter, they *(meaning the systems)* face not an evolution, but an overhaul. The Great Divide will quickly mark the players and their purpose for all to see. Choosing to work with one over the other will be obvious and absolute.

Your new Earth is built in transparent collaboration. This as opposed to secret control. It is a joyous process, my dear human.

We will speak of this again.

That is all.


*Thank you.*

# June 15, 2021

It is the One.

Things have happened that are worth noting. The timing of them. The blatant nature of them. These things have to do with your transportation methods and systems. The systems that run them.

You've come full circle.

By this is meant that the controllers who've held the controls have become those who are controlled by their own creations. It is an irreversible process, and a re-occurring one for them. They (the controllers) have a very old, brilliant and limited playbook. It's been utilized in other places, on other worlds, and with other races. It purports to account for every possibility. Yet it has a major shortfall. It (this playbook) does not account for any new development outside of its box. The box that holds its instructions.

These are heralded as relics – priceless secrets passed on, once having reached elite status. These are not meant to "keep up" with evolution, adaptation or change. In fact, one of the major shortfalls of these sacred methods is their refusal to consider evolution as possible.

Repetition is their downfall.

Expectation creates a scenario that for them, includes a limited and specific set of possibilities. It is why the playbook is known and familiar. Many star seeds, light workers, light walkers, light warriors and truth tellers remember. It is always the same.

# Words of One

What is not considered is adaption. What is ignored is learning.

Libraries are destroyed to prevent this from interfering with their plan.

They are not prepared for an enlightened race, and this, my dear human, is who you are.

What has reversed and locked them in, is their own plan. It depended on secrecy, on hidden people, programs, paths, roads, documents, alliances and purposes. All of these held beneath the matrix. The matrix they built; slowly, gradually, purposefully and relentlessly.

So slowly, as to be unnoticed by the majority of the race.

Those that noticed, and came to warn you, were isolated and could be removed relatively easily and without too many questions.

What was not accounted for was the current combination of celestial movement, energetic influx and global awakening. The moment is poised for the big reveal. There are things that do not add up, have never been clarified, and are now about to become transparent.

Your world will only go forward with complete honesty. Nothing false carries on. The light forces will no longer consent to perpetuating dark agendas in order to limit societal upset and/or reaction. Deception has no place in your new world.

What has back-fired is the build-up. The sheer volume of what has been kept from the public is approaching society with the force of a tsunami. It cannot be stopped and once it washes through, there will be nothing left standing in its wake.

**The lightworkers emerge then, in full radiant and active mode. As the devastation and truths revealed wash over all that you know, your role is to remain standing. Hold on to those who seek comfort.**

Even you who have been told of the depth of deception here, will not be fully prepared for its reach. None of you have the full story. With grief comes the process of full acceptance.

Nothing changes until the reality of what "is" is accepted as truth. Denial will carry on for longer than you believe it should. Realize that it is not up to you to decide the timing for your brethren's journey. It is up to them.

You will find yourselves in places that seem to tempt that. There will seem to be obvious answers to problems. You will want to take over and implement these answers.

Resist the urge.

This is more than a correction. It is a permanent fix that must be comprehended and completed "hands-on". It is the only way to ensure that there are no repeats.

Your human history on earth is about to be written by the population of its members themselves, in their own hand, recording what they themselves did or witnessed. The reasons behind each doing or undoing will be included and documented.

# Words of One

It is no longer the age of Monopolies, Big Brother, Big Government, Big Pharma or New World Order. It is the age of the New Hue-Man. Hue-Man 2.0 is birthing on the ashes of slavery.

All of what emerges throughout the birth canal is necessary. Not all of it will be around for long. Yet, it is part of the process.

You are about to participate in the birth of a new age of Man. As with any birth, it is painful, messy and miraculous. It will bring you to your knees in wonder.

That is all.


*Thank you.*

**June 16, 2021**

It is the One.

There are things to say.

These things concern who it is you are now, who it is you imagine yourself to be, and who it is you are in the midst of becoming. For I tell you they are one and the same. When you comprehend life without linear time, you will see this.

No doubt, you witness remnants of this now.

*Please explain.*

Certainly.

There is a sense in which you are never surprised. This is due to the fabric of your origin that is with you always. Your core truth. Your essence.

There are times and lives that ask you to forget that essence. In such moments, which may span years or even centuries, you've willingly "put it aside" in order to pursue other, more separate and difficult learnings. You've, at these times, seen yourself isolated, disconnected and unaffected by the remainder of the race.

All of you have completed this cycle.

# Words of One

It is why, and this is uttered with the deepest respect and utmost love, it is counter-intuitive to assume arrogance, "better-than" or "holier-than" another of your race.

For you have been each other.

You have been every other.

In a very true gesture of love, you will appreciate the sacrifice being offered by those who chose the dark hats for this time of the final act.

They knew this role included their exposure. They took on the task, put on the suit, in full awareness of their end-game, their full exposure.

The selection of such a role requires deep love for and faith in humanity.

They took on these roles knowing they'd be hated for them, eventually exposed in them, and having to face the human consequences for them.

They did so to push forward this moment you arrive at now. They do so in a more and more obvious format, in order not to be missed. **They are supplying the fuel for the fires of Ascension.**

It is not your imagination that their dark efforts appear more and more obvious. It is by intent that this is so, even if it is subconscious intent.

For those of you on the earth right now are here with purpose.

That purpose rises to the surface of your life more quickly as you move into the coming new season.

The Season of Exposure and Disclosure awaits.

It is your next turning.

You've all prepared and are ready.

Who you become, will not be that much different from who you are right now. The fabric of your pure essence will not disintegrate in these coming times, although it may look different. Its strength will be tested and you will be proven unstoppable.

All challenges are to be met by you, have been met by you, will be met by you. You are Gods in training. You will soon see clearly the other Gods by your side.

Their costumes and their roles will not change their core. Their identity is equal to yours.

You are One.

That is all.


*Thank you.*

# Words of One

It is the One.

There are emotions coming to the surface now. These may have a lot, or little, to do with facts as they emerge. Facts as they are disclosed, as well as details that are exposed, coincide with, **yet are not directly caused by,** each other. There is a saying: "correlation is not causation", and this applies now and it applies here.

Your flood-gates are opening in more ways and places than one. It is time for everything to be made known. Everything that was once hidden. This implies everything about your society, as well as everything about you.

You will notice new frequencies, unknown abilities and surprising conclusions that will occur for you – seemingly un-asked for and (also) at your command.

The truth emerges on all levels.

The truth emerges in every earthly arena.

The first place you will witness these truths are within.

The spell-casters are receding and their effects diminish as they do.

What happens, as a result, is that the spell-bound become un-bound and either un-hinged or free as a result. In either case, and eventually, they'll breathe in more steadily and recognize their truth more readily. It matters not whether or not they recognize the spell.

It matters that they recognize, ultimately, the truth.

There are old ideas surrounding justice and who is right or wrong that will have to be wiped away and forgotten. This is the beginning of an entirely new world.

It will be built on truth — not on rules and laws and machinations of control.

It is the frequency of truth that enters now. It is the frequency of truth that exposes all —

All that you consider dark

And

All that you consider light

Right now.

The truth of what you are capable of arrives into your field at the same time that the truth of this fabricated reality does.

You are well-equipped for this.

Remember that.

All of you are. Some of you will have to be reminded. Some of you will choose not to remember, despite all evidence presented to the contrary. From this point on — **choices are all self-driven.**

Remember.

# Words of One

It is not your job to coerce or convince others of the "right" choice or "true" belief. It's all been cooking long enough and it has come to a boil.

You are up to the choosing.

You've made many preliminary decisions leading to this one. Yet — and it will help you to remember this — for it is true in every case — changes can be made at any point.

**At any point.**

You cannot know the inner workings of a soul. You are only privy to your own.

These coming times will include shocks and revelations and sadness. All of these temporary conditions of the human heart.

Feel them through and through, and know that you will react now and mourn for things that are new to you, but not to mankind.

The horror and abuse that has been done to the race has been going on for multiple ages. It has lived on due to secrecy. It ends now.

So, do not mourn for long — you have come to eradicate the darkness.

There is a new world to construct. It will be built on love and hope and collaboration and unity. It will not be built on fear.

Unity celebrates love and is the trademark characteristic of the earth human.

So, welcome the frequency that enters today and breathe it in slowly. Allow it to surround the forthcoming announcements. You may be tempted to fall into despair right along with your fellow humans who are not forewarned.

Do not, as it will delay your progress and take you off course. This is the beginning; it is not the end.

What you are witnessing, in these announcements of things and endings of things is akin to the ashes that form beneath the Phoenix as it rises.

There are necessary deaths, closures and final moments. All happening in preparation for the rising of the new.

This is a cleanse. This is a destruction of all that is false, so that the things that are true can emerge.

You've come to live this moment. You've come to be transformed by this moment.

You are here to transform a world.

It is done.

That is all.

Now the fun begins as you try your wings.

# Words of One

*Thank you.*

**June 22, 2021**
4:33 AM

It is the One, Sophia.

There are subjects to consider.

These will help to explain what it is you do and how it is you feel when you are confronted with anomalies. These are things that don't follow the narrative or behavior you've mostly known. These are things that do not fit current explanations or definitions. They show up, new to your awareness, asking then to be defined and explained.

There has always been a plan, an over-riding voice of control who decided and explained the story of your life. This story supplied you with some sort of logical sense for the matrix.

It became your science. It told you why you saw certain phenomena and together formed your story.

*Note – This stopped without explanation. I suspect I fell back to sleep, due to the early hour, which was noted. It is included here because it was an interesting explanation for how narratives are formed...*

# Words of One

**June 28, 2021**
5:30 AM

It is the One.

There are things to say. Yet you have questions.

*Yes. Thank you.*

*Will you talk about the vaccine?*

They are meant to be instruments of death. They will not do what is their intended purpose, but they will inspire a great deal of fear — which by itself is the cause of much suffering. Some will die. Not the numbers hoped for in the overall plan, but in great numbers. Numbers that will alarm the populace and force a hard stop to the program.

Remember, all who have left here are making a choice to do so. There are methods of protection.

There are methods of healing.

These will become widespread and well known before much longer.

The race does not suffer to the extent it was intended to by the oppressors.

Their plan has been halted.

They are done.

It is time now for rejuvenation and healing. There will be relief of grief. There will also be joy.

The time to rejoice is near to you now. It waits around the corner of exhaustion. You will see.

*I must stop.*

Yes, Sophia.

# Words of One

**June 30, 2021**

It is the One.

There are things to say.

It is time for you to hear these things.

It is time for these things to be written.

However, recall please, the moments experienced now of anxiety and withdrawal. They all matter. All of this matters. The time you are in right now is like no other before it. It is a time with no precursor. History has not been told in a transparent enough way for you to prepare for such a time as this. You have not been prepped. Not been told the truth. These days have not been walked by the human beings before you.

**You are the first.**

What we will offer then, is some guidance, for it is lacking. We will present it in a way that will allow for it to be interpreted by any branch or race of humans. We will present an overall picture.

For what is it that happens now?

**You do.**

All that you are capable of – you become.

This is not metaphor. [10]


These are not words given to cheer you up or pull you along. You'd ask (if they were), and rightly so – "to what do you pull us along to?".

It has been a very long journey, my dear, dear, human. So very long.

There has been no pre-determined ending or promises kept while you walk this earth. There have been promises of riches in the "after-life".

These words are here to tell you that life does not end. Therefore, do not hold out your expectation for rewards or riches "after". It is all now.

There is only now.

You are here to experience a physical transformation while manifesting a physical vessel. You are meant to embody every second of this shift.

You knew, before agreeing to participate, that it would be a challenge for you. You knew you'd have to ad-lib and you knew that there was no instruction manual.

These words will have to suffice.

---

[10] *a figure of speech in which a word or phrase literally denoting one kind of object or idea is used in place of another to suggest a likeness or analogy between them (as in* drowning in money*)* Merriam-Webster

# Words of One

They do not list specific instructions. They are more like suggestions or guidelines, and they are a bit more fluid.

There are not hard or fast rules for this. You may design some of your own — later. That will be up to you.

Initial exposure to all that has changed, will feel negative to you. It will be a challenge, because of the last eighteen months, to believe or accept anything that is new, as potentially positive.

Some things to keep in mind as you proceed are these —

-Until now, authority has been pushing its own lethal agenda, and hiding it beneath unfulfilled promises, smooth talkers and money.

-You are used to trusting these voices and have ignored or disabled internal discernment.

-This does not imply that all smooth talkers are untrustworthy. It is to ignite your internal discernment.

-You have always been slaves. Slavery propagates fear and obedience and a tendency to look for authoritative voices before acting.

-You will have to become your own authoritative voice.

-As **One**, you are embodying **Oneness**, yet this does not imply Global Authority. It implies **One Voice.**

-You will hear that voice in small communities, individuals

and countries. What you will hear is sovereignty. What you will embody is self-confidence.

-There is but one unifying principle and it is love. It is love. Love is what unites you and binds you to one another. It is the spark you feel with contact. It is the chill of recognition. Both indicate self-awareness.

-What is happening now, as you walk on the earth and dream in other places, is that you are becoming self-aware.

-It is the reason for the destruction. All that is not true falls away. All that is not you leaves, to make room for you – to give space for true – **to allow love.**

-**Fear cannot withstand love. Release your worries and watch what takes their place. It will always be love.**

-This may feel uncomfortable because it is new – not because it is wrong. Fear not the new. Look upon it with clarity and eyes of discernment. Evaluate and decide:

Does it separate?

Does it unite?

For it is only the latter that survives now. Only the latter that promotes freedom. **Freedom is your current destination. Make no mistake.**

There may be very loud distractions and very shiny new roads that tempt you to go elsewhere. Remember.

# Words of One

Remember your destination.

It is freedom.

It is collaboration.

**It is for, not against, each other.**

> **Does it unify?**

> **Does it separate?**

All subjects can be answered with those two questions.

Ask them often.

The days ahead will give ample opportunity for you to do so.

That is all.

*Thank you.*

Goodbye Sophia. My chosen one. My scribe.

# Words of One

# Chapter 3. July

# Words of One

It is the One.

Things have occurred on your planet. These things will illustrate for you a change in control. These things will illustrate for you a shift in the command structure.

It will appear as if no-one is running the show. While in fact, and finally, those who are more publicly holding power positions are on the side of humanity. They begin to publicly orchestrate the removal of the dark forces.

It is as if there are shades of dark. Some deeper than others. I tell you; it is such a time for the race of man, that all forward movement for him will come from the light. This is inevitable and the only way.

Creation moves to balance herself now, and in order to do so, must do it with an influx of light. This light must exceed the dark. Its force must propel the dark from this place.

This is formidable. This is unstoppable. This is how such darkness, that has held its grip on the race for such a long, long, time, gets replaced.

It gets replaced with awareness, power and intent.

It evaporates with consciousness.

The force of a fully awakened human will no longer succumb to any dark doings.

It is man's purpose – now – that he takes his place at the controls. On Earth. It is destiny.

What you will witness is military involvement. What you will hear about is crimes coming to light. You will seek justice for these crimes. They are crimes against humanity.

Justice will be served.

Know that in these days, the final days of life as you've known it, no stone is left unturned. Mankind will see to this.

Mankind will see to this.

What happens next is an outing, then a cleansing, then a re-birth.

What feels overwhelming now will very soon become hopeful. Some of the race will more quickly adopt a hopeful countenance, it is true.

Yet I tell you that swiftly all of you will. The energy of love assures this. Light guarantees it. For both move quickly and with more power than fear and dominance.

Fear and dominance are like the schoolyard bully here – they may look and sound scary, yet their ability to run things depends on that which is the opposite of truth – which is fear. They are all show, without substance.

# Words of One

Love is what sweeps through now and it literally surrounds you as it also comes from you. This is a moment of complete immersion and no one escapes its effect.

It is why you see so many who seem to be falling apart. They are losing their grip on "reality"; when their "grip" had some basis in fear.

With the eradication of fear, they do not have anything holding them together. In fact, they must hold themselves together and they must do so with love.

They must do so with love.

Nothing false will proceed successfully. Nothing fearful will withstand this next phase of truth. For this is love. It is your absolute truth, and is what takes command now.

You will be breathless at the speed in which this turnover is completed.

You will experience jubilation.

It does not feel that way today, as you witness the disintegration of all that is false.

Know that your fellow man is, right now, responding to the world as it is currently presented to him. It makes little sense – with truth, deceit, corruption and camouflage currently in one place. It is a mixed-up place indeed.

What you offer and what is needed now, my dear, dear human, is consistent and persistent love. You are One.

It is the ultimate truth that reverses the trend of domination and lies here (*on planet Earth*).

It is Oneness that ultimately becomes the voice of Man. The Singularity is where your truth is discovered. One voice. One core Truth.

What feels to many like a "breaking apart" is a "coming together".

Offer yourself as the glue. Be the love that you are, in every circumstance. The stability of that Truth will ultimately unite you all. Unite you each to One another. Bring you together, as One.

That is all.


*Thank you.*

# Words of One

## July 6, 2021

Sophia, it is the One.

There are many subjects as we move forward through this season of alteration. A year ago, you participated in a season of preparation for what happens now. What approaches and what is occurring will become, one day, the point in time when everything changed.

You are still in the midst of preparation, but the moment is almost upon you.

For this has been said before, yet it is worth repeating here and today, that there is a point at which it all changes. There is a moment in "time".

All of you have seen this moment.

It was the full experience you reincarnated for, and what you signed on for.

It begins now. The turmoil and uncertainty you've felt these last 18 months will, quite literally, move, to include the ground you walk on, the place you live, the earth herself.

For as the dark extricates itself there is room left for movement. There is space. Things shift. These that are shifting have been what you may have considered immovable forces…

Death and taxes

Rocks and land

Banks and the elite

Monarchies and institutions

There will be so many upheavals, my dear, dear human, that to feel overwhelmed by them will become the new normal. You are each overwhelmed, particularly those among you who reinforced their identity from society. The entire societal structure was built on illusion. It has been held up with media and hype, glamour and money.

It is a false structure and will fall.

It is a false structure and will fall.

There are many well-meaning people who make a living while utilizing this false structure to support them. They will either fall or seek sturdier ground.

For the only thing that remains after the preparation and the alteration is truth. It is the force that holds you together.

You, the strongest of the strong.

You, the souls determined, this time, to rid the planet of the slavery system which has held her for centuries.

For you know what it is to be free.

# Words of One

You know what it feels like to love purely.

You know what brilliance looks like and remember autonomy.

You have felt your power always.

It is time, my dear, dear human, to re-capture the essence of creation that enlivens you, and supplies the rhythm to your heartbeat.

It is time.

We have been speaking here actively for many months and will continue to do so. Hearing these words is meant as a reminder for you. You chose to come.

You chose to live on earth, right now.

How you found your way to these words is not the point.

The point is that you found them now, and for you, the timing is perfect. You have given yourself these words to assist.

You have never been alone. Your generosity of spirit and tenacity of spirit has kept you right on target.

It will be worth every step taken.

There are no delays in creation – all occurs in perfect synchronization and will fit together in an audible "click" when complete.

It will be unmistakable.

You are in for such a treat.

Trust.

That is all for now.


*Thank you.*


Goodbye, Sophia, my chosen one.

# Words of One

**July 13, 2021**

You are entering a permanently changed reality. It changes
gradually. As the pedophilia pipeline ruptures, the banks collapse,
and as they do, the money stops its free-flow into all of those
(*humans*) taking part.

It blows wide open and all at once. While most humans will
struggle for their necessities and to make sense of this news that
they are hearing – the participants in this most hideous evil will be
gathered up and/or running for their lives. Money and reputation
will be the least of it.

*I see chaos…*

Yes.

It will be very frightening and quite confusing. Heroes will arise
then. Awakened ones to calm the fears of the sleeping ones. Such a
time on Earth has not been seen.

You are living through the end of times. This is not the end of you.
It is the end of times. These times. The time of the enslaved
human race. It is ending. **All must be in order before it does.**

Prosperity for humanity is part of the plan. It has always been part
of the plan.

In such a time as this you will be faced with multiple and frequent attacks to your reality. This is because it crumbles before your eyes.

As it does, bits wear off here and there. At first occasionally, then it will feel like an onslaught of strikes against what you have known as real.

These may look like any or all of the following:

> Your body may suddenly or periodically feel or respond differently.

> Your dreams will no longer feel "other-worldly". Yet more as if they are running concurrently with your physical life.

> Nature will change in ways that you haven't seen before.

> Your desires will shift.

> Your eyes will see differently.

> Institutions may dissolve, many, for sure, never to return.

> Your concept of time will shift.

> Your ideas around value will get shaken up.

These are the obvious shifts. You may not perceive them at first as any big deal. An ache or pain, here or there, a few closings, some odd weather patterns. Yet eventually and relatively quickly, these will accumulate and patterns of alteration will be perceived.

# Words of One

It will help to discuss the vast length of "time" this Awakening seems to be taking; linear time that is. For there are some of you (*who are*) reading these words who've waited decades for its arrival.

The shift in consciousness and change in frequency was seen by your seers and known about long before now. What feels imminent has felt as if it was on its way for a very long time.

It is now in your lap, you might say, and as you get up and move around you are feeling it.

"Why is this taking so long?" You ask.

An entire civilization is being adjusted. Parts of it are being eliminated. Many of its deepest inner workings are coming apart on their own, or else they are being forcibly dismantled.

Your reality has been based on a construct that was designed to hold you always in its grip of enslavement and subservience. It has no intention of letting go and is right now being forced to abandon **what it can no longer control.**

This idea is not one it believes; it therefore will hang on until it sees the futility of doing so.

**Your reality is changing this way because this is the way you are changing it.** There are a lot of you working together to do so. Many do so without full clarity as to what it is they are changing.

This all takes time. Time determined by man. Time also determined by Source, who will enter the scenario at a certain point. There will be no doubt of this moment. There will be no questioning this moment. Your reality will be forever changed once it occurs.

You will not miss this.

You will not miss this.

That is all.


*Thank you.*


Goodbye, Sophia, my chosen one, my scribe.

# Words of One

**July 14, 2021**

It is I, Sophia. It is the One.

There are no words that will satisfy this ache your heart bears. It is an eternal pain, born of centuries of heartbreak and disappointment. Such is the life of a human. Such is the mark you wear.

Wear it proudly now, my dear, dear human. For you have come now to end the torment, to rid yourselves of the suffering, to expel the darkness that captures your dreams and invades your history.

These are tasks only taken on by the brave and you, my dear, dear human, wear that mantle now. You've put it on yourself and willingly kept it, knowing of its discomfort. You are a singular force, a soul to be reckoned with, a warrior for ultimate truth.

In the end, once this act is said and done, there will be those among you standing tall, observing the wreckage of a once-captured race, and asking yourself "why?"


Now begin the explanations.

These start before the end completes itself so that you appreciate fully what has been accomplished. These start as you walk through the process of the ending.

Humanity began as a thought, an utterance of physical expansion. Love in tangible form.

Once experienced, identity emerged. Expression defined it. Desire for more added depth.

Infinite life thus emerged and as this accompanied physicality – it came coupled with conflict.

Preferences arose.

Strengths followed as favorites were repeated. Each of these layers raising questions and investigations, inquiry and deep dives into possibility.

Tastes and pleasures and distastes and displeasures, all magnified and quantified and separated then again.

Each exploring… All of it play.

Until emotion leapt out and showed itself, right alongside expression.

Choice became knowable and its potential manipulated.

For always, there were originators. "Early birds", who'd been playing far longer than others and who now desired a larger playing field… Much larger.

As diverse ideas emerged, so did levels. Levels of knowing. Levels of experience. Levels of ability. Levels of desire.

There arose a question of right and wrong.

# Words of One

There arose ideas around the permanence, the sanctity, and the purpose of all of this playing. After all, we were expressions of thought really. Utterances of physical expansion. This was a game. A game of exploration. A game that always led to expansion.

**A game we were playing.**

What were we to do?

As consciousness developed, experience provided myriad opportunities for yet more explorations and manipulations.

Explorations of the physical matter we were playing with.

Explorations of the mental ability it was using to get around the game. How much could we change?

How long could it last?

What would happen if we ___ (fill in the blank)?

Are there unspoken considerations we should add to the game?

The concepts of fair, conscience, and free will emerged.

There are differences of opinion about who was consciously playing this game and who were mere players — unaware that there was a game at all.

For sure there was tinkering and combining of traits. Most certainly there were differences of opinion. Divisions arose on every level; every single level.

The divisions didn't stop the game. It only changed how it was played and where.

The game continued.

As eternal expansion moves every forward, the game completes itself. It has out-lived its usefulness. No further learning continues, regardless of how long the game is played.

I'll repeat that, for this is where you are today.

No further usefulness is achieved in the playing of this human game — therefore it will be stopped.

The reason it will be stopped, and make no mistake here for this stopping does not come from an angry God or a judgmental God…

This stopping comes from the inventors and players of the game who have seen it played to its conclusion and are no longer learning, expanding or growing. These inventors and players are you, dear human.

You, right now, have many players who will not stop playing. They have forgotten it's a game. They think this is real and that this is all that there is.

There is so much more.

**It will seem as if there is judgment,** because those that play still, have broken so many rules of the game that there is only one way

115

to stop their continuing.

It is through an act of power and display so forceful as to be **unmistakenly not human.**

In fact, this act will be brought forth, instigated by humanity and you are almost there. Almost there.

That is all.


*Thank you.*

## July 15, 2021

It is the One.

There are things approaching you now, things moving into your field of vision, that are reaching you in order to raise the alarm bells. These things have to do with what is happening in your skies. These things have to do with what you will not hear about, not be told about, but actually witness.

They are not what they pretend to be. They pretend to be threatening and unexpected and dangerous.

They are none of these things, but instead performances meant to appear as if they are real.

It is not the purpose of these writings to raise alarm or inspire fear. Rather, they are meant to inform.

Sometimes the information shared is frightening by its implications. It is always truth. It is always real. It will come to be realized that what has been exposed in these volumes of words has been humanity's true history – nothing more than what occurs for the race.

You are within a long, drawn-out moment of disclosure. These words can be said now, because they are true. It is as simple, and in some cases, as hideous as that. You have not been told these truths, yet at the same time you've been kept focused elsewhere, on make-believe frightening things. You've been looking at them for so long that they've become believable. You've been looking at them specifically so that you wouldn't look at other, more terrible truths.

# Words of One

You expect an alien invasion. It will occur.

You do not expect your favorite celebrities to be feasting on children's blood – yet they do.

Which is the more horrifying truth?

Which have you been kept in the dark about?

Do not be so single minded as to dismiss out of hand things you've never considered.

Retain an open mind with a full heart and both real and false will reveal themselves to you.

That is all for now.


*Thank you.*

# July 21, 2021

It is the One.

You have questions.

*I do. Thank you.*

*They surround the information I was given yesterday. It concerns the timing of the Ascension, the timing of everything. A year ago, you gave me markers to watch for. Would you expand now on the information from yesterday and the markers and where we are? Thank you.*

Yes. You find yourself much different than you were a year ago, do you not?

*Emotionally, yes. Physically, yes.*

You will notice subtle changes first. Remember this is a singularity. One cannot be separated from the other. One aspect of you does not exist in isolation. It exists as a part of the whole. Always connected. Much like humanity.

What you notice now is exhaustion on many levels, and a quiet, in a sense. It is not that you are quiet, but that the urgency has quieted. With that exhaustion/quiet comes a certain acceptance. These are what have been coined "stages of grief". ("**You are ending a time, a world, a moment, a matrix, a way of life.**" *These words*

# Words of One

*came as I was transcribing, which has never happened before. It seems as if One has become my editor as well!*) First, there is shock. Eventually comes anger, denial, negotiation/bargaining and eventually – acceptance.

What you notice is a sense of commonality, a coming together as well as individuation. You are seeing others for who they are, while noting the common thread that binds you – regardless of opinion.

The point in mentioning any of this is to signify the change from just one year ago. Then, there was a general feeling of chaos and out of control. There was physical separation. There was physical violence. Anger. Shock. Fear.

Today, although to some degree you find this still, another feeling accompanies it. There is also a sense of acceptance; acceptance of differing points of view. There may not be understanding or agreement. Yet, there is acceptance. Not one of you has not encountered disagreement with a loved one/important "other".

That has helped to facilitate this "pause". This room for new thought. It revolves around the notion of importance and the concept of value.

What becomes primary? What would you place at the top of your focus? This last year and a half have honed your point of view. There is less insistence on being right.

**You are beginning to comprehend actual unity and true Oneness.**

This concept is one that must be lived. It is being felt viscerally now, and lived out quietly in your families and amongst friends and associates. People of value to each other, who share some aspect of their identity – yet do not agree.

In this climate this cannot be avoided or ignored. Your earth life has become a shared experience due to the released virus and subsequent reactions and efforts. You are looking at the same thing – although through your own lens certainly.

**This process will have to be lived.** There is no way to explain that to your satisfaction as you go through each day. **You live it right now**. It accelerates in progress as you do, and although there are no precise indicators such as mileage or percentages, certain things have to take place before it completes itself.

That is the reason for the markers. They hold today. You notice that some of them have occurred while others have not. [11]

There are facets of this journey that remain hidden to you. As it proceeds, you'll have to find voices that you trust to point the way. Some things you are hearing and seeing are deliberate miscalculations. Others are mistakes. You will find a few who attempt to deceive you, even now.

If things are said to you that invoke extreme emotion in either direction – take a second look. Deliberate manipulation of human emotion is the #1 tool of the dark ones. In this way, you are weakened, kept off-balance, distracted. A focused and empowered human is not something they want to deal with.

---

[11] *These markers were noted on July 22, 2020 and can be found in Words of One, Volume II.*

# Words of One

To summarize and clarify and to answer the questions posed here, the markers remain. They are not, however, meant to be taken in sequential order exactly. Think of them as cumulative. They will have to occur in order to fulfill the process.

**You begin now to Unify.**

You will have to come to a collective decision. This has not yet happened. Once it does, things will rapidly proceed. In this way, the metaphor is accurate.

Remember that set-backs and propulsions can and most likely will occur at any stage.

What holds true is that a decision to participate in this inevitable process was made by each of you before birth. What will be lived out, felt and realized will be the part you play in it as it completes itself.

It is the richness and fullness of your human emotion that drew you here in the first place. There are things to be gained from this moment that you won't want to miss.

The reason these things cannot be precisely foretold in a linear fashion is because you are deciding each moment as you live it. Let me repeat that. **You are deciding each moment** as you live it. Billions of you will collectively decide how this moment proceeds. The fact that **it will happen** is not in question. **How** is up to you.

That is all.

*Thank you.*

# Words of One

**July 22, 2021**

It is the One.

Everywhere, there are changes. As the earth herself fluctuates with the change in frequency, so do all participants on her. Systems, machinery, people, vegetation. Even your air responds and in doing so, alters everything that breathes.

All life responds to this shift. All life cannot help but be affected.

It is an agreed upon arrangement.

You'll see. There will not be long-lasting or detrimental effects to everything that's decided to stay.

As you adjust, remember the choice to be here for this was made freely. Made by you.

How you live through it will be self-determined. This is the way with all of life.

You are One. The shift happens in every corner; each nuance of life is impacted. Whether recognized or not, you all feel this.

It happens now and now and now and now. All changing in a continuous fashion. Evolving as you alter form – altering as you evolve. One beautiful, cyclical process.

Next you will notice movement. Movement of others.

Many gather now. Show up to watch the show – "Earth in her final days of control". There is no way to keep these onlookers away.

They are riveted.

You may be seeing them already, out of the corner of your eyes. Just the corner. Once you do, turn to look in their direction. Let them know that you know.


*Here I was interrupted and had to stop. This conversation was never completed. Sophia*

# Words of One

**July 23, 2021**

It is the One.

Things have come to pass. There are events that signify the end of times. Some of these have been seen by humanity's seers. Some of these noted already by the people

The coming of one of these things is the subject I wish to talk about today. The coming of an event that has been noted by several of humanity's seers. This would be the floods.

When the floods occur, and they will, it will be helpful to remember that all locations and levels of participation are chosen beforehand. Before occurrences in linear "time". Before being experienced. It's all chosen beforehand.

The floods will appear catastrophic and climactic, as indeed they are. They are also natural responses, stemming from nature recycling herself.

Some of them have been expedited due to man's actions. Others have been delayed. There are, in some cases, decisions made to push things in one direction that actually push them in the opposite direction. So, although there has been deliberate man-made intervention that is causal in these floods, it will not always be immediately clear which are which.

The waters will flood, of this you can be certain. It is not a punishment from God when they do. It is an act of natural consequences. God will not punish.

You do not quite grasp the enormity of what happens for you as a race and the planet as you stand on her. It goes way beyond the scope of human responses to injustices and crimes. So much further beyond that.

The scope of this coming moment will be evident to you as the powers of nature are engaged and respond.

The fact that these physical responses correspond with the emotional and intellectual responses, along with societal upheaval and change, is not coincidental, yet also not the whole point.

**You are One.**

This Oneness expands beyond the race, beyond the race and the planet, beyond the galaxy. It extends to all of creation.

This coming moment – signified physically by the floods – occurs simultaneously beyond time.

What you have on earth is a front row seat where you'll see it, feel it, hear it, sense it, smell it and know it in every facet of your being.

This is not metaphor.

You will come next to a point where the only focus will be the Event. As Gaia rumbles and undulates and moves and waves – so does humanity.

The timing was inevitable. All things resonate with Source. It is not causal so much as cooperative.

# Words of One

You will witness synchronicity as it is demonstrated globally. Both worldly and other-worldly sights, sounds and movements announce to you the Event. You will be listening by that point. Do not fear.

No one misses this next moment.

That is all.


*Thank you.*

**July 25, 2021**

It is the One, Sophia.

Realize now that you are witness to the end.

What will emerge before it concludes, is everything. The exact nature of this cannot be foretold or predicted as if on a schedule. Some of the elements, you've been told. All of the elements, you've seen – before this current incarnation. Before this now moment.

*I am having such a challenge remaining conscious throughout these conversations recently. There is so much information. There are so many pictures.*

An attempt will be made to ease up during contact, yet I tell you this – you are in a dense period of time. There is so much to transmit and within each subject is a multitude of subjects. You are a conduit. Once you open the gate, it is as if a flood swells and that is overwhelming to your spirit. My gentle one, it may help you to initiate contact along with the most alert time of day for you. Also, to prepare and be ready for supplemental things to keep you alert and focused.

*Do you mean coffee?*

If that is your preference, then yes. These will not slow down or become less dense. You will have to remain focused and alert throughout.

# Words of One

We are no longer in casual conversation. We are in production. There are reports to be made and they are most helpful when they emerge near to the time of their release.

*You are saying these can't be eased up?*

It cannot, not as it was in past times. You are changing with these times. Yet this process moves along faster than your physical body can keep up with.

*This is good to know.*

*Let us continue then?*

Yes.

We will stick to a single focus. I realize there are many in your head and visions – yet we'll focus on just one.

Also, this process needs to be daily for a while.

*I've been feeling that, yes.*

We will return to the subject, the subject for today. For it is the beginning of the ending and at this point, there will be many reveals.

In a very natural way, you've deduced the ending on your own. Let it be explained in this way.

Time, in actuality, is not linear. It is an active component of physical existence and it continues non-stop. It is circular, inclusive and continuous.

The reason that all of this will feel familiar for you, as it occurs, while it occurs and when it occurs is because it is a part of your life. Your choice has been made to experience this.

How do I know this?

Because you are reading these words, and it is happening for you now. Regardless of your exit plan – you are experiencing this shift. It happens now.

You will know when it has reached its conclusion. **Nothing will be the same at that point.**

At a cellular level you are being altered. At a spiritual level you are awakening. At an intellectual level you are becoming enlightened. Your emotions are changing.

All of you is already in the process of responding to this shift.

Do not be in a rush to get to the "end". The process you live through right now is the richness, the juicy part, the things you've come now to live through.

# Words of One

You are discovering your awareness of each other, your potential for compassion, your potential for generosity, your understanding of self.

This does not mean the same for each of you.

This was your epiphany Sophia [12], and for today we will focus there.

It is a similar scenario to the future timeline story that you are

---

[12] *A few days prior to today's conversation, I had a sudden realization, an epiphany, complete with a visual of what the end would be like for us, for all of us. This happened while driving. It was not as I had pictured it to be. We do not all end up with the exact same quantity of information one day.*

*Life just continues. Things get massively more peaceful and love filled and prosperity abounds yet the entire race does not quite note the moment that this changed or why. They do see governments and institutions change. They do notice the improvement, and they may notice that there was a moment when something massive happened globally. I'm not sure of that part.*

*There are some of us who are aware of this happening and watching with bated breath, while others of us are focused on other aspects of life here. This is as it is meant to be. All of us are necessary; some of us came to see that the Awakening happens on our watch. Like anything else, how you experience this moment depends on your current perspective.*

*This matrix has been constructed while utilizing our limited attention spans and associative tendencies. This shift is happening to the entire race and will operate in a similar fashion.*

familiar with. [13]

In a sense, those of you here for this change, those of you here to assist and propel and promote and speed up this change — are from the future.

You came here with a mission. It is yours. **It is not everyone's.**

You will be sitting together at the end of all of this, and recalling a much different journey. Many of you are already there now, with loved ones and associates who seem to be looking at a much different world than you are.

This will not be any different in the future. You are here to help with this Ascension. You will succeed. Your progress does not depend on the percentage of humans who know precisely what is going on and by whom. Your success and the speed with which it is achieved depends on your light. That is it. You are here to spread the light.

Yes, things will be revealed and truths will be told. Yes, some of the humans who chose such a role will be arrested. All to facilitate comprehension.

Eventually, the story will be told.

The story will be told and recorded and remembered. It will not be repeated. Not here.

The lessons incorporated in this process of Ascension are many. Most stem from experiencing personally whatever has been your

---

[13] *The Tomorrow War*

chosen role.

You are seeing a focus on judgment. There is a desire for punishment administered for these crimes against humanity. Humanity will make that call together.

Some facts will emerge, not all, but enough. Validation of these so-called "conspiracy theories" will happen. Yet only to a point.

Each of you will confront your personal judge and jury as you proceed – as was mentioned earlier – the beginning of the end starts now. You will each experience this end **through your own eyes.**

**Pay attention.**

Your heart speaks louder now than it has ever been allowed to. It won't be stopped.

When this is over, you'll find a gentleness and a peace in even the harshest demeanor.

This is true transformation. Be patient with yourselves. Be kind to one another.

Love emerges now from all of life.

There are no requirements. Everyone participates, regardless of where they end up.

That is all.

*Thank you.*

Goodbye Sophia, my chosen one.

# Words of One

It is the One.

*Thank you.*

You are noticing how now, "in broad daylight", the efforts at enforced compliance escalate and multiply.

There is not a clear-cut way to respond to these efforts. Not if you believe them to be valid and based on reliable men and women of good intent, with the well-being of mankind at the heart of it. The demands are confusing and crazy making. Once they are recognized for what they are, they appear preposterous and obvious.

Yet realize that not everyone sees them in truth, or for what they are. You cannot convince those that do not, that they are anything other than what they are told that they are. This denies their reality.

Such a doing must come from within the man or woman themselves, and not from outside. Such a doing is self-discovered and most typically springs from the same source which introduced the confusion in the first place.

It is here where I will begin today.

Some, many, of your fellow humans have come to participate in the final act and be part of it during the big reveal. These players are as yet unknown to you.

You will discover their parts once they begin reversing their behavior. You will know them by what they do, when they do it, what they say, and when they say it.

It becomes important for you to recognize the big picture here. As you watch the show, remember, it is inevitable and continues until its conclusion. Regardless of set-backs, missed lines, wardrobe malfunctions or stage fright. You are freeing a planet.

There are last minute stand-ins, waiting in the wings, for every player and each scene.

The show must go on.

As you witness it, note the participating level of every player; including your own. It varies, yet all are imperative.

Some of you chose particularly brutal scenes which caused irreparable damage – either to yourself or others. How this determines your response now is yet to be seen. Yet you can be certain that for each player, both their lines and the scenes they participated in were chosen before-hand.

What this means, my dear human, is that you cannot know the heart of any other – not during the play.

Let me say that again.

You cannot know the heart of any player, or define its purpose, while making that decision based on their human actions.

**This is a play.**

You are fed lines and you play parts according to agreements, lessons and ego.

**You are One.**

Yet the parts played during this final scene will shout that you are on opposite teams.

**You are on One Team.**

It is this illusion that you came to see through. It is this fabrication that you came to identify. It is this matrix that you came to dissolve.

**You will do so with light; with your light.**

Some of the brightest and bravest among you are hiding in the dark right now. They will exit before you recognize their brilliance. The pain of this role has cost their soul dearly. This does not excuse their actions. It defines Oneness.

There is but One Love.

There is but One Light.

There is but One You.

That is all.

*Thank you.*

Goodbye Sophia, my chosen one.

# Words of One

It is the One.

You've come now for current information. You seek help. There are things that you would like to see foretold or explained. This is the nature of physical life, the nature of the race.

There are no simple answers, as your experience is self-examined and personally defined. Yet global transformation holds some of the information you seek and today we'll start there.

Some of the changes you are proceeding through now can be defined in that arena. What supports this is the general tendency of the race, of both races. For there are two diverse races participating now as lead performers. Both are known.

The game plan for the aggressor, which in this case is the non-human race, has a play list of actions that are known. These have been studied by the humans who are orchestrating the current take-down.

Human response is a known variable for both sides.

It is to your disadvantage, as you attempt to make sense of and determine what will happen next, that you do not hold the same level of content that is available and used by either side. You are participating in the show while being blind-folded.

The best that you can do is to guess, based on what is deemed most possible. Here is a bit of insight that will assist.

*Note – this transmission stopped at this point, and was never returned to or completed. There are times when the content, for one reason or another, is too much to handle, and the force of it acts as a sedative, making it impossible to remain conscious. This was one of those times. I'm sorry about that, as this one sounded promising…Sophia*

# Words of One

It is the One, Sophia.

There are subjects to consider discussing. We have as yet to broach the subject of heredity. Heredity as it applies to lifetime chosen. Particularly chosen for this upgrade of the human organism while occupying a human body.

For your body exists as its own component of you. The holder, if you will, of your soul for this incarnation. You would be different in multiple ways if you chose instead to occupy another body.

The reason you are unique for this lifetime, in all of creation, is because of the combination of your ancestors and eventually your parents **at the moment of your conception.**

Then, you chose a specific time to enter your mother's body, which is where you were forming. What forces propelled you to enter when you did? Was it moments, hours, days or weeks before birth?

It all matters and combines in order to shape you now. This life. The one you are creating.

What happens in truth is that you end up resembling your ancestors because you know them. In many cases, you've lived with them before.

Soul families can, not always, feel more similar to physical families, because in truth you've shared not one lifetime, but many. In physical families there are skipped generations. Yet you'll do so as a group (*typically*).

There are patterns and they feel familiar.

There are struggles and they feel familiar.

How it often works is that you will arrive together to help each other out. Your lives are inter-twined in more intricate and complicated ways than I can describe – each component of this is unique to the soul and its relationship/agreement with the corresponding soul. This could be brother, sister, mother, father, grandparent. Even further "back" than that.

There are some of you, especially in this now moment, who feel completely foreign in your family of origin. It could be, in that case, that you basically "hitched a ride" so that you'd be where you are right now.

It could be that you are here for a very specific lesson and/or to provide this for another.

Once an incarnation occurs, your family of origin grows. It is like you are then not only connected to each other from soul memory, but from body memory.

Do not discount this.

You are a physical being with an eternal soul. Both have history, connections and impact the person you are becoming. [14]

---

[14] *Equal is what came to mind most powerfully. Both physical and soul parts are equally participating in who it is that you are right now. Physical family is not to be ignored or brushed off.*

# Words of One

It will help to research your ancestors. They have secrets to tell you about who you are, what you are capable of and why you are here now.

You are unique, yet not unknown. All of you are connected.

Each of you has a purpose and generations of ancestors who helped you decide what that purpose would be.

You are helping to transform a world. All of your parts are needed. All of your talents and skills will assist when the moment arrives.

**This is true of every body.**

**This is true of every soul.**

You came for this transformation and have been planning this for generations. It is time to accept all that you'll become. For until you see the end result as a possibility, unless some portion of it isn't imagined by you, dreamt of by you, or known by you – it will not manifest.

This new world won't be **hoped** into existence, it will be seen into form and created as real by Masters. These Masters are here. These Masters are you.

It is time to accept all parts of the past and really look at the future you are here to usher in.

It is time.

That is all.

*Thank you.*

# Words of One

**July 29, 2021**

It is the One, Sophia.

There are things to notice. Things it will help you to be aware of. Consciousness implies awareness and there are truckloads of topics of which you are not. Part of this conversation will help to inform you, to introduce ideas previously not considered relevant.

This does not imply stupidity or dullness. It signifies the conditioning and control to which you've been subjected.

It is all that you have known.

It is time for new ideas and further considerations to be put into old ones. It is time for new thought.

You are constructing a new world, and this one has your best intentions at the very core of it. This, my dear, dear, human, has not always been the case.

For you do not move backward in time, but forward, ever forward. By this is meant the purpose of new information is to propel the soul. The soul follows one direction and that is towards its own evolution. It is a slow, circuitous route, and the length of "time" spent on any single moment is self-determined.

The purpose of adding today's bit of information to your resources is to increase the scope of your vision. For certainly, if you have been following along so far, you have expanded your view. Yet there is always more.

Do not make the assumption that at any point you hold the complete story. There is always more.

Todays "more" includes the idea that there are some of you who've been specifically planted in places quite public – working for one "side" – while actually assisting another.

This holds in every case, all institutions and for every subject matter. Many of them, and listen carefully now, **do not realize whose side they assist.**

These come by their words honestly and believe them to be true and necessary, whether or not this turns out to be the case.

It is here where you'll see and hear things that don't add up. They appear confused and sound confusing.

This, my dear, dear human, is a specifically chosen role. Not all of what you see is a "white hat plan" or a "dark hat plan".

The percentage of you who consciously realize that there is a plan at all is relatively small. You are the ones that agreed to be conscious and aware while helping.

Others, many others, agreed to help while remaining mostly unconscious throughout this part.

This part was shown to you all, and you knew how messy it would become. We've spoken of this earlier in a more general fashion. That was in the 2020 year.

# Words of One

These are the helpers who will be swept away and loudly so, promoting what for them is an obvious and necessary point. Until they experience a dramatic shift, and they will. This shift is not to be escaped and it involves the race.

When this shift moment is internally felt for these "plants", it will have with it a very obvious and loud change of viewpoint.

Remember, that at this time, you will not evade yourself or your true calling. No-one escapes inner truth. Those that cannot hold it, may succumb to it and exit. Most will not.

The reason to mention this now, is to encourage acceptance and discourage judgment, based on what it is you are seeing and hearing from all of the players. They may be plants, they may not. Yet the point is, until this is over, you will not know.

This is not over, and this applies to all that comes from any other into your sphere of awareness. Whether family, associate or journalist or government official or medical official.

You'll know when it's over.

All cards will have been played.

The final card is as yet played.

Inner trust and connection to your core truth is vital for you now. Above all, stay in touch with self and respond accordingly.

Stay away from judgment.

You'll know soon enough.

That is all.

*Thank you.*

Goodbye Sophia, my scribe.

# Words of One

**July 30, 2021**

It is the One.

Completion approaches. You sense the nearness to it now. An ending of such magnitude that it is felt throughout creation itself. Hence the anticipation.

Hence the many and frequent "announcements" of pending action.

Unsure of precise details, yet aware that you reach ever closer to culmination - there is a good deal of chatter. Many "false positives", if you will.

You all sense it. For some of you, it feels like doom. For others, jubilation. No-where can you seem to find the complete and honest truth — the full story.

This, my dear human, is because you are creating this right now. Within it are 8 billion scripts and outcomes. These must be merged until that singular moment is reached. [15]

The moment arrives when it answers all of the possibilities. There will be something in this moment that works for everyone. Each of you will resonate with it at some level and you will know. Know that this is truth.

---

[15] *Seeing a rolling screen — searching for anomalies — a rolling screen of numbers — kind of like a betting machine, waiting for the row of cherries or dollar signs to show up at once, a "one-armed bandit" slot machine.*

This is what is referred to as "Divine Timing". For there is not a single God in the sky, rolling the roulette wheel, and deciding when it stops.

There is you.

One.

A single force of love and light co-mingling and contributing to a single thought. That thought could be:

Freedom

Or health

Or prosperity

Or joy

Or compassion

Or assistance

Or magic

Or a miracle.

There is a moment, and you are almost there, when you will find that connection and **BAM!** The Event, Universal Abundance, Overwhelming Bliss, Mind-blowing love, and Compassion to Enormous Proportions. All at once. Everyone's prayers answered **at the same time.**

# Words of One

**You Are One.**

This is the secret they've kept hidden from you.

They cannot. You feel now and hear now the cries of the children and the pain of the trafficked. Your eyes are on the entire world, via the internet, and this speeds up and strengthens your connection.

Divine Timing is determined by **you**, dear human, by you. It is why it becomes important to maintain your focus on what you desire most to witness.

**How will your prayer get answered?**

See that.

Feel that.

Hear that.

Imagine that.

It is your best contribution and it cannot be taken from you. This, they cannot stop. They've tried and continue to try, with non-stop rhetoric. You've seen through the illusion, and break-through is imminent.

It is imminent.

You are sovereign beings with free will. You make up your own mind. They attempt to make it up for you. It is a farse and a part of this final act in the show.

Your contribution is whatever energy you offer. The frequency supports you now.

You are a bringer of light.

Divine Timing approaches more rapidly when more and more of you are on the same point of the dial.

They can distract you. They cannot change your mind. You are in complete control.

Use every tool at your disposal.

Intend.

Believe.

Allow.

Expect.

These do not require money or anything physical. In that sense, without requirement and beyond time itself – it is done.

You are but One.

That is all.

# Words of One

*Thank you.*

# Chapter 4. August

# Words of One

**August 1, 2021**

It is the One, Sophia.

The subject today considers not time at all, but the concept of the absence of time. It is a critical concept to the visual for our previous conversation. The spinning wheels of thoughts.

*Okay. I am receiving images.*

Go on then.

*It was more like ideas really. Ideas about the wheels of thoughts having no specific "time frame" attached to them. Sort of an eternal spinning slot machine, where the wheels/thoughts spin 24 hours each day and for 365 days each year – year after year after year. It stops (an individual wheel) on a thought or realization of sovereignty;* **it just stops spinning.** *Then it waits. It is waiting for the other wheels to stop as well.*

*The other wheels keep spinning though. Eventually and ultimately, they all stop when an idea of sovereignty is thought of, and then held and owned.*

Yes. And some of these have been stopped for decades. You would call these truthers, whistle-blowers, star seeds or warriors.

The thoughts continue, **but the wheel stops when truth/freedom/awareness/sovereignty is realized.**

Everyone will get there. This moment is like no other in that the wheel is held in place and visible by the current frequency.

Everything changes now.

This is how time enters the picture.

Time has no effect on the event. It (*the* event) is the literal manifestation of an authentic, fully realized human. There is a visceral component of this that transcends time.

You are within a cushion of love and light that will hold, maintain and transmit each sovereign moment. You are becoming One.

This has not been possible before now.

Everything changes now.

Your visual showed you dates, calendars and people with them. They were combined thoughts from past, present and now. Each now is new. Each wheel continues.

The event is not that all of you have the exact thought at a specific literal moment in linear time. Linear time is not real in the concept of creation. It is circular, inclusive and constant.

Yet, my dear human, you live in a dimension that is ruled and organized by linear time. There are future "thoughts", future feelings and realizations that echo sovereignty – and **the wheel stops when that happens.** *(The collective wheel, which is all of the individual wheels, each of them holding still with a thought of sovereignty.)*

# Words of One

In your current place, earth 2021, these wheels have yet to reach that sovereign idea. They will.

This is seen from a place that is not run by linear time. They are seen and noted.

The event is inevitable. Freedom for the human on earth in 2021 is realized. This occupation will not be successful, and it is near to its end.

Come now to a place of comfort and spend your linear "time" imagining your new earth. This, my dear, dear human, will increase the speed in which it manifests before you.

There is no other way for you to impact others. Their thoughts are their own and their wheels will stop at the moment they actualize sovereign. Not a bit sooner. Not a bit later. It will happen right "on time" and "at the perfect time".

This, my dear, dear human, is divine timing.

You are so much more than you realize and hold all of the controls in your very own hands.

You will see.

It is done.

That is all.

*Thank you.*

Goodbye Sophia, my chosen one.

# Words of One

It is the One.

There are subjects to consider and reasons for them that are necessary to discuss.

You begin a rapid moment in your race's history; in Gaia's history. Time accelerates. The processes that cannot keep up with this acceleration will be abandoned. This is a trip of choice and also of function.

What you will discover as you move forward is that many of the procedures which your society asks you to engage in, are not meant to evolve with you or to assist you. No. Instead they were invented to hold you up and stifle the process of unfolding.

Unfolding occurs as an opening up – not a closing down or covering.

Things are revealed in an opening.

Surprises await.

Discoveries are made.

Sometimes things have to be unsealed.

Sometimes things have to be taken out or removed.

Comprehension happens gradually with an unfolding. It is a step by step awakening to potentials that lie dormant or have been hidden.

You are unwrapping the vast expanse of your heart, and witnessing the brilliance of your light unleashed.

This is not meant to shock you with its force, but to embrace you in truth and tease out the authenticity that awaits. It is there. It is you. It has always been you.

As things speed up, try letting go rather than hanging on. You sometimes hold on too tightly and this impedes progress. A first step will have to be taken. You cannot fly if you insist on remaining in the same place. At some point you will have to trust.

Speed is not something to fear. It is something to adjust to. As the frequency increases, things happen closer and closer together in linear "time".

Realize that your frequency increases as well. The speed of you has no limit. It is only in this 3D physical realm that such limits are perceived and accepted and adhered to.

Not so elsewhere.

Remember, this is a unification of sorts. Many of you have had dreams in which you are flying. These are other yous, other versions of you, other aspects of you.

It's all true.

It's all you.

# Words of One

Things disappear at times from this frequency because they've inadvertently moved into a speed that in invisible here; here in this 3D realm.

Things move in and out of your visual field for the same reason. You sometimes perceive more realms, from deep relaxation and connective states.

These will increase for you now as "time" speeds up here.

Days/hours/minutes move closer to each other as you proceed with a mindset that watches clocks. There seems to be no "time" to rest or slow down.

You approach the ending.

You will simultaneously begin anew.

You will not physically perish in order to change states of being. "You" will remain "you" throughout. Only there is more of you present for the part as it were. It will be a complete experience, a joyful reunion, a moment long anticipated.

As you proceed through these upcoming days, pay attention to everything. The whole of creation carries messages and it is a promise that if you perceive something in any fashion – then there is something in it for you – a lesson, a message, a reminder. This is a time like no other for you my dear, dear human.

Let go and allow. The journey will be so much more enjoyable once you do.

You are in for such a treat.

That is all.

*Thank you.*

# Words of One

**August 4, 2021**

It is the One.

There are things transpiring now that bring to light some of the darkness that has been ongoing for you here. They are, what you might say, "in the works". This is not to say that they are new, as the process is ever-unfolding. This is to say that developments have reached a pivotal point and, quickly now, there will be full exposure.

Full exposure of truth. Full exposure of fact.

The darkness now moves into the light. The activities that have been conducted in the darkness now move into the light. Into the light of exposure, where more of the race will have access to them. Where more of the race will see them.

These are so heinous and inhuman that they sound fake, and are just not mentioned. It is too much to talk about for most of the race who hold compassion for every other.

It is an unimagined horror, and takes the mind "too far" to be considered real. "No one would do that".

Yet, that is its purpose; it becomes invisible by remaining unreal. The switch from unreal to real is a tough one to make. In some cases, an impossible one.

Realize that the years of misuse of the human have not helped. The level of degradation and pain and horror only creeps out in occasional films and books. These are then dismissed, and the "owners" are pleased. For in order to satisfy the magic requirements, the magic must first be announced.

Shows like Hunger Games illustrate the truth. The truth of your world.

You are about to learn how much of it has been horrific. There is not much regard for the human being, not within this group.

If you consider the way your bred animals (*livestock on factory farms, not family pets*) are treated, that holds part of the insight into the ways humans are treated. In order to realize the full picture however, you have to add on a few things.

These include:

This plan is thousands of eras in the making.

This plan has been perfected elsewhere.

This plan has been hidden, until recently, from humanity as a whole.

Out in the open now, the plan's movements are blatant. To the person, the specific details (**of what is done to humans on a regular basis**) are beyond imaginable. Humans would not naturally do these things to other humans.

When the specifics are known, it'll be clear that these are committed as **acts of crime against humanity.**

# Words of One

Everything changes with clarity, and the plan is destined to fail.

Literally consider what this will mean for the race. This is a time like no other. The light is bright, all gets exposed, there are legions of warriors and all of creation supporting and propelling this moment.

The realization of it and full acclimation to it is solely yours however. As members of the race, you are embodying the horror as well as the brilliance.

It's taken quite a bit of "time".

It's taken quite a bit of intent.

You enjoy, and right now, the energy of creation behind you.

You will not do this quietly or alone.

It is to be spectacular.

Yet, and here is the hard part, my dear, dear human. You must live through it, see it through until the end, and feel it.

Feel it all.

You are cushioned through this with your higher self and your highest good directing your movements. You will not have a difficult landing because of both, yet it will not be easy.

It isn't meant to be easy. It is meant to be accomplished.

The stories of the children, the races, sacrifices and uses will be painful. Today's message comes to assist with that moment.

When something shocks you for its inhumanity or horror – breathe deeply and send peace, gratitude and love to the soul who endured this horrific act. Then, let them go and see them for the brilliant light that they are.

This is how they want to be seen. This is who they are. Grief and depression and further pain **will not assist.**

Only love heals.

Only love.

Remember, as announcements and revelations come into view – love will get you through this.

You will have to be strong. You are up for the task. You were built for it actually. Generations of you contributed and still do.

This is not "too much" for you. You are here for just this moment.

That is all.


*Thank you.*


Goodbye Sophia.

# Words of One

It is the One.

We will continue now our journey along humanity's path of discovery. It is seeping out everywhere and seeping out for everyone. Discovery is part of the human protocol. It is why you incarnated at all.

To be alive and human is to gain insight into life; its purpose, its truth and your purpose in having one (a life).

This is part of the reason why you must not fret about this truth emerging or that false story being told to the population.

If it is true, it will remain so.

If it is untrue, it will become very obvious — obvious to everyone.

There are reasons for the journey through a false narrative. These have to do with growth, expansion, evolution and also, in some souls, a karmic attribute is present.

Many of you sense this last part now, in your current time.

Karma is not payback.

Karma is not punishment.

Realize that at a soul level you are One. At your core truth, you see the equality of every life lived. You recognize the purpose and cooperation of each lifetime.

It is not as simple as "your sins are forgiven". That is a way to express an idea with a deeper complexity to it. Living a lifetime requires the cooperation of every soul involved. Living a lifetime is not done without purpose or preparation.

All souls participating in and affected by the life lived, **have, on the deepest instance of their existence,** agreed to this.

There are no exceptions.

This implies that the concept of "sins" being "forgiven" is an erroneous one.

For if everyone is equal – just who is forgiving who? And if everyone agreed to the roles they played beforehand – then has there been any "sin" committed in the completion of a part? A part chosen by you and sanctioned by everyone who knows you?

"Sins", in their true sense, could be a term used to indicate specific and conscious actions that are taken **for the sole purpose of benefitting self – at the expense of another human life.** These are human acts. These include what you call "crimes against humanity".

The karmic sense that is felt now, is regurgitating up because you are remembering who you are.

You have been it all. You have done it all. In some way or another, you will feel it all, now.

# Words of One

You are not sinners. You are human. You are here now to assist in the awakening of the race and the turn-over of the controls. If you are reading these words, regardless of when or how, you have come now to remember. To remember all of who you are. To remember all of what you've done. To remember it all.

There will be no stone left unturned or life left untouched by this upheaval, reversal and return to love.

What will be, what **is being** let go of, are concepts of sin and guilt and judgment.

You've been told to fear God and to obey.

You've been lied to, in order to gain control over your very mind, your own body, your individual life.

You've been lied to.

You are not here to be punished.

Yes, there are actions, and many, that will stop now. They must, for they are based not on love but on fear. Fear is a falsehood; a captivating, mesmerizing falsehood and it is the last remaining weapon in an arsenal of control weaponry.

You dismantle fear with love.

You disengage fear with intentional light.

You dissolve fear with truth.

Fear is no match for agape.

It is time now to utilize this moment of truth, absorb all that it is telling you about yourself and embolden your actions with authenticity. You are invincible once you know who you are.

It is advised that you reduce all media now and increase peace in your days.

These are the final days before the switch. They will appear chaotic to those looking at old lines and expecting them to be repeated.

Nothing will remain the same after this.

You are here now to see to that.

That is all.

# Words of One

Sophia, this is a time of change. Most certainly a time of systemic change. What will result from current reversals and directions will flip society over. This will not be immediately evident. It will resemble chaos.

It will help you to remember that in fact it is a necessary step in a planned insurrection towards the guard. Chaos precedes order each and every time. There are no massive changes possible until current processes are disrupted. The disruption of society feels chaotic.

It will help you to remember that the chaos is necessary, and ultimately leads to a more palatable and comfortable system.

Your entire way of life has been underlined with destruction and harmful intent.

All of it.

Your food, intentionally poisoned.

Your medicines, intentionally harmful.

Both, intentionally addictive.

Your money becomes harder to "earn" and less valuable.

Your government serves its own agenda, one you have never been told.

Your entertainment is a form of mind control, complete with its royalty and riches.

None of the current society serves your best interests.

None of what you've been told is your history is complete or truth.

This is a necessary crumbling.

The gift of a physical rising, an Ascension while occupying a human vessel, is in the moments now felt.

Never again will there be a lack of understanding in you regarding:

Anguish

Discrimination

Fear

Manipulation

Lies

Pain

Control

Grief

Unity

You are becoming One in all ways and to witness your

# Words of One

transformation is a glorious privilege indeed. [16]

That is all for today.

I am complete.


*Thank you.*


Goodbye Sophia, my chosen one, my scribe.

---

[16] *The visual here was of an enormous sunflower. With its center the focus, and each of the black dots/seeds representing humans. It was enormous, obviously alive and actively forming. The petals were in place, keeping the seeds/humans gathered as One. Most of the center was complete, with all of the humans/seeds gathered together in the center of the circle. Yet there were blank spots and some humans/seeds separated off by themselves, away from the large black center group/majority of seeds/humans.*

*They were isolated and felt unsure of themselves and fearful. It was over 70% complete, not quite 80%, yet it was increasing as I watched. The seeds/humans would suddenly run away from the isolated groups and join the larger one.*

*Point of view was as if I was in an audience, a galactic audience as I felt all of creation watching humanity with joy and laughter and popcorn! These were the emotions that came with it. Each time one of the fearful or separate seeds/humans ran over to the larger group, there were "oohs" and "ahhs" and cheers from the audience. This was beautiful and joyful to witness. What a show!*

## August 7, 2021

It is the One.

There are things to say. These things concern your current situation. The unrest builds and it builds relentlessly. It will not stop building until something is resolved.

Hear this.

There is an inevitable resolution. This is a one-way journey. It heads towards a culmination, a release of tension where items are ultimately resolved. Many and all unanswered items are answered. Many and all uncertain subjects are settled with certainty in this next moment.

Do not expect to see a slow-down of tension. See instead change. See instead resolution. See answers given. Then imagine the satisfaction when freedom ensues. When prosperity arrives for the race, as was intended.

What is happening is a build-up to an ending. It is a conclusion that answers all queries.

The appropriate parties are identified for the parts they played. History is re-written. Sinners and heroes are revealed and, in some cases, re-labeled.

It is a heady moment indeed. One in which the whole world in engaged.

You feel this building now. It cannot subside. There is an inevitable

# Words of One

ending and it is followed by a glorious new beginning. This must be how it goes.

The pace quickens now, and there are alarming announcements and broadcasts of fear. Recognize the spell when it is invoked and reverse it with truth.

Reverse it with love.

The ramping up will not stop. It will be dismantled and dissolved with light.

This is an energy battle, as those who believe they control the race cast their verbal spells – those **who actually do control this moment (this is humanity)** counter-act with refusals. The spells themselves boomerang.

Your best action now is non-compliance.

Your most powerful action is stillness.

The thing to say no to, is anything attempting to stifle your personal power.

The war will be won with love.

The war will be fought with light.

Remember, there is no such thing as a "dark". Dark is an effect. It shows up when there are no lights turned on.

**Turn on your light.**

**Turn on your light.**

**Turn on your light.**

That is all.


*Thank you.*

# Words of One

It is the One.

Now is the time for a re-telling of what occurred here, here on earth.

For the story will be told, and it is for the best that there are accurate tellings of it. You will count these words among those accurate tellings. There are others. All of which will rise to the top as cream rises in a bucket of fresh milk.

Man was never meant to be a slave.

Man was never meant to be trod upon by any other.

Man was and is a hybrid, a "mutt" as the term goes for your canines.

Man was not an experiment. He was a process; a beautiful collaboration of attributes combined with this planet's native species.

Something new resulted, and thus began the ownership wars for control of Man. For he was a gem and the earth is a jewel of a planet. The combination of both was irresistible.

The Reptoids eventually and most recently dominated and are the group being evicted now – in this present moment.

They no longer occupy quite so much of the control grid – but there are many, still beneath them, carrying on as if it is the only way.

What becomes important for you to comprehend is the sheer beauty and wonder and potential of Man. You see, my dear, dear human, this potential could not ever be erased. It didn't matter who controlled what eras – the diamond within the core of the race remained.

Evolution and the unrelenting spirit of the race continued always and now, right now; it is Man's moment to shine. The gem will be revealed and what you are capable of is known in stories of mystics and magicians, Gods and prophets.

It is time for you to shine.

It is your heart that engages your inner light, and activates the power that has always been yours.

Your success is inevitable, yet there is effort still. You will need to actively participate and you are not used to such activity. You have been convinced of your weakness instead of your strength.

This was intentional and unnecessary. The controllers are no longer directing the show.

This next act is yours.

There are messengers of peace, prosperity, love and truth everywhere.

Soon – theirs will be the only words that remain around longer than the effort it took to say them. [17] This is because of the frequency. It has changed and will continue to change until the shift is complete.

Once it happens, it will be like shutting a door on a murky, confusing, dark and fearsome place and walking into a new world. Fear and manipulation and control will not be found in this new world. It is built to support itself, and is, in fact, self-sustaining. It is collaborative. All of its parts support life.

Life.

The human is revered in all of creation because the human **is from all of creation.**

The Reptoids considered ownership and rule of the race a feather in their cap. They will pay the ultimate price rather than give up such a hard-won position.

This is how they think. It is important for you to know that they've transferred this inborn tendency into many of the humans who do their work. It's become a group of staple characteristics – greed

---

[17] *Visual here was of words disappearing in the time it took to reach the audience. It was of a speaker, telling lies to a large group, and they heard nothing from this woman although she was dressed in a suit and considered herself important. The words she spoke "fell on deaf ears" as the people literally heard nothing and instead were engaged in their own gathering, looking at each other and making plans for how to proceed, for what to do next, and for what was needed. The words literally disappeared due to the fact that they were not truth. This woman and her lies had no effect.*

and dominance and control at all costs.

Some of these are physical hybrids: Reptoid/Human. Not as many. The personality traits are/have been transferred without every physical attribute.

You will learn so much as some of these who've worked closer to the "top" speak.

There will be no surrender. For there is no new leader *(to surrender to)*. Humanity will now speak for itself.

There are things you'll wonder about. These are around issues of "who is who?" and "who can I trust now?" and "are there any hidden still?"

I tell you this.

When the ending of this matrix occurs, it is a complete closure. The door shuts. The frequency shifts.

Those players, **all of them,** who still desire to continue in the denser, manipulative, power-over frequency, **will not be in the new world.** They will not survive the shift or the uptick in frequency, and this is by choice. Their choice.

Do not concern yourself with the players who remain. Yet, this does not mean return to "laissez-faire" attitudes and letting a small group of individuals do all of the deciding. There will be work to do for all of you, and plenty of it.

Remember the lessons learned under the strong-arm tactics of

# Words of One

Reptoid control. Remember so that they can be a part of your new history and retained as things never to be repeated.

They will serve then the purpose they were meant to. That will be to forge the steel of a brilliant and unique being who volunteered to forget itself in order to discover and experience the contrast – Dark to Light – The blackest night to the brightest dawn – The weakest collapse to the most powerful rising.

Your time to rise is upon you.

Fearlessly embrace this change, for it is yours and has been lovingly constructed by you – by all of you.

Each tear, every life, all of the pain and all of the joy have been part of this construction. Your new world is you, my dear, dear human. In all of your realized brilliance and actualized love.

You have yielded an abundant crop and your harvest awaits.

That is all.

*Thank you.*

## August 10, 2021

Sophia, what troubles all of you now is enhanced in your field by the encroaching energy. It moves in relentlessly, and as it does, your status-quo is upset. Sometimes turned upside down.

Very quickly now there will be a need for answers.

Soon now there will be a calling.

Many of the star-seeds and warriors are feeling this already. It is as if they have a longer hearing range and although the precise moment is not right upon you, the need for you to be ready for it is. They hear this calling now.

There will be a need for calm and re-assurance and you will provide this. It is important to prepare. The saying "It's just like riding a bike" applies here.

Once your body learns and holds the positions and actions for bike riding, you only need to be back on a bicycle for you to remember them. It is a body memory.

What occurs for you now is a soul memory.

You are about to engage. It is a process you've engaged in prior to this moment. Prior to earth in 2021. Other rescue missions were performed by you then.

You have not needed these particular skills for quite some time. You have never needed them while human – until this now moment. Earth in 2021.

# Words of One

You will remember. It is body, heart, soul and emotional memory. You will experience total recall and will, at the moment you are needed, know without a doubt what you came to do.

You'll remember why.

You'll recognize who you came to do it with.

The calling begins.

Some of you feel it in the distance as it approaches. Some of you know it in your bones. You will not miss your call.

What helps you at this juncture is an uptick of energy, a speeding of frequency. Your memories reside there also.

Do you see?

Your entire world shifts now, and as you flip and shift with her – your frequency does as well. You remain together.

The Earth and her occupants are entering a new realm. Together. Right now.

You will let go of your denser attachments. You will need to, there will be no choice. For you have come to liberate a planet and her people and you will have to fly.

The wisdom with which you will enact your part in this story will astonish you.

"Where did that come from?", you'll wonder. Initially.

Eventually, perhaps all at once, you'll remember where it came from. You'll remember it all.

For you are a bringer of light, a keeper of the flame. These things are who you are. These things are what you do. Specifically, and soon, your part will be clear to you. You'll remember. It will.

Once it does, it will be like riding a bike. You may encounter steep hills or flat tires or bumpy roads, but you've done this before. And you've done this multiple times.

Trust your heart and seek its wisdom often. The moment approaches and you'll hear your calling soon.

That is all.


*Thank you.*

# Words of One

Sophia, it is the One.

There are things to say to end this volume.

They are to be recorded here and the volume is to be produced.

There is some urgency to its release. In the coming weeks you will be busy for many reasons. Not all of them concern this volume. There are others. I will address the others now.

In all of the predictions there have been mentions of "days of darkness". Darkness literally means the absence of light. The phrase has been uttered and passed on from era to era, each one in various states of advancement.

"Darkness" in a world prior to the electric light holds a very different meaning than it would now, for you, on earth in 2021.

Darkness now also implies a halt to connection, to communication devices and the internet. There are multiple ramifications.

For this conversation, we will throw all possibilities for light and physical connection into the category.

There is meant to be a moment of darkness.

There is meant to be a return of light.

It lights up and connects you in a new world.

Your world, this world, as it is currently run by those who feel they hold all of the power here, ends permanently with the darkness.

This is what comes next.

The darkness hails the new world.

The darkness closes this chapter. It does not end your physical life; it shuts down the matrix.

What comes next is wondrous, gorgeous and beyond description. It is meant to be a surprise.

You are prepared.

You are prepared.

Whatever shows up as the darkness – know that you've gotten where you've intended to go all along. Stay clear of fear.

Stay away from panic.

Refuse to awfulize.

Stand your ground.

**Hold the light.**

**Your new world is seeded with your light. This is your purpose.**

# Words of One

**It is fed and nurtured and blossoms with the incoming love.**

There are surprises coming your way and this is how you've chosen this to be.

You wanted an Ascension while human. You'll have exactly that.

This will activate your forgotten gifts and start your new life, your new world.

You will know when this occurs.

You'll know why and how and who you've ever been. You'll know who you are supposed to ever be. You'll see your life with crystal clear vision and immediately grasp your potential.

You'll also see the truth in everyone else.

This moment has been crafted, manifested and now will be experienced by you – by each of you individually. There are no mistakes.

Ground yourselves.

Center yourselves.

What approaches is a brilliant reversal and obvious truth.

The explanation for the darkness is obvious once it occurs.

There has to be an illustration of what occurred here. A demarcation of the moment when it all flipped – **Darkness to**

**Light.**

This is no small or insignificant doing. This is a collective acknowledgment of Oneness and it breathes in love and exhales light. Freely, purely and absolutely.

It is to be noted.

It is not to be forgotten.

The days of darkness approach.

What comes after will astound you.

You are in for such a treat, my dear human, a well-deserved treat.

Trust.

Love.

Hold the Light.

You will see.

That is all.


*Thank you.*

# Words of One

# Words of One

# The End

Made in the USA
Las Vegas, NV
13 October 2021